HOW TO
Handle THE
Hard-to-Handle Student, K–5

This book is dedicated to my son
and business partner, Marty Appelbaum,
and our entire Appelbaum Team. I could not
do what I do without the backup of this incredible,
dedicated team. Together, we make great things
happen for children and for all those
who are in their lives. Thank you.

HOW TO
Handle THE
Hard-to-
Handle
Student, K–5

Maryln Appelbaum

A JOINT PUBLICATION

CORWIN
PRESS
A SAGE Company

Appelbaum
Training Institute

For information:

Corwin Press
A SAGE Company
2455 Teller Road
Thousand Oaks, California 91320
www.corwinpress.com

SAGE Publications Ltd.
1 Oliver's Yard
55 City Road
London, EC1Y 1SP
United Kingdom

SAGE Publications India Pvt. Ltd.
B 1/I 1 Mohan Cooperative
Industrial Area
Mathura Road, New Delhi 110 044
India

SAGE Publications Asia-Pacific Pte.
Ltd.
33 Pekin Street #02-01
Far East Square
Singapore 048763

Printed in the United States of America.

Library of Congress Cataloging-in-Publication Data

Appelbaum, Maryln.
  How to handle the hard-to-handle student, K–5 / Maryln Appelbaum.
     p. cm.
"A Joint Publication with Appelbaum Training Institute."
  Includes bibliographical references and index.
  ISBN 978-1-4129-6438-8 (cloth : acid-free paper) — ISBN
978-1-4129-6439-5 (pbk. : acid-free paper)
1. Problem children—Education. 2. Behavior disorders in children.
3. Problem children—Behavior modification. 4. Children with
Disabilities—Education. I. Title.

  LC4801.A67 2009
  371.94—dc22

2008020180

This book is printed on acid-free paper.

08 09 10 11 10 9 8 7 6 5 4 3 2 1

Acquisitions Editor:	Jessica Allan
Editorial Assistant:	Joanna Coelho
Production Editor:	Appingo Publishing Services
Cover Designer:	Monique Hahn

Contents

List of Figures

Chapter 9

Foreword

Maryln Appelbaum is a remarkable woman. Many of you do not know that she was a high school dropout. Yes, that's right; she was a high school dropout. She grew up in a home of poverty and chaos, was a student at risk, and became one of the hard-to-handle students she writes about in this book. But she had a determination that helped her succeed in spite of the adversity in her life. She was a teenage mom, had two children, and then beat the odds by returning to school to not only finish her high school education, but also to start collecting university degrees and a teaching certificate.

Her studies and her life were always about children. She earned master's degrees in both education and behavioral science. She completed doctoral studies in education and psychology at two universities. She has worked both as a therapist and as a teacher. She found that her real love was teaching hard-to-reach students, and, at one point, she opened her own private schools and packed them with students who were "special." She earned a reputation for being able to find ways to handle each of those students so that when they graduated from her schools, they had something special within them, a gift of knowing they could succeed. When she started those schools, she did not have students who were labeled ADHD, bipolar, LD, Asperger, autistic, or OCD. Yet many of the students she taught came to her schools because they had been expelled from other schools. Many had all of the above labels, but in those days, those disorders were not identified. When these students came into her schools, they were viewed as special challenges, challenges that could and would be met with successfully.

Maryln, in addition to writing books, speaking, and helping run the Appelbaum Training Institute, writes thoughts for the day that go out to educators around the world. In one of her recent thoughts for the day, she wrote, "You just never know the difference you may make." She then went on to tell the story of a woman whom she had recently seen at a holiday party. The woman said, "You probably don't remember me. My son came to your elementary school. We brought him to you because we felt hopeless. He had been labeled mentally retarded at his other school. They said there was no hope. You found the keys to his learning. You gave him the confidence he needed. He saw that he was not mentally retarded. You showed him how he could learn. My son just finished his last year at college. He is now a chemist. I want to thank you."

That is just one of the countless ways Maryln has helped others, which is what makes this book unique. This book is not only packed with strategies for success, but it is filled with Maryln's stories that are success stories—stories that you will identify with, stories that will motivate you to use the strategies in your classrooms. It is a book filled with strategies as well as hope. She believes that with the help of a caring teacher, children can "beat the odds."

This book is also unique because it takes the different special needs of students and offers a strategy-based book on how to handle those needs and those students. It is a book that will benefit not only educators, but all people who work with students, including doctors, psychologists, social workers, counselors, and school administrators. The book will also benefit parents. It is more than a book on behavior management and on discipline; it is a book on how to connect with every student. It incorporates psychological as well as educational strategies that can totally transform your classroom and the way you teach.

I want to share with you one more story, and it is a personal one. Maryln Appelbaum is my mother, and I am one of her success stories. I struggled in school and was a challenge to teach. Most of my teachers gave up on me. One went so far as to tell my parents that I would never do well in school. I would never make higher than a C and would never be able to attend college. My mother didn't share this information with me and instead vowed to prove to me that I could achieve anything in life that I wanted. In fact, she taught me that I could help others instead of feeling helpless. She taught me to lead instead of needing to be led. She instilled in me the love of teaching. She is an important voice in the lives of hundreds of thousands of educators across the globe. This book is most certainly the best guide of its kind ever written.

Marty Appelbaum

Preface

It was the '90s, and people were all talking about the number of students they had with attention-deficit/hyperactivity disorder (ADHD). I was working with my son, training teachers in classroom management, and everyone wanted to know more about ADHD. I did lots of research, contacted other authors, and attended conferences on ADHD conducted by psychologists and psychiatrists. I even contacted drug companies to find out more about the research on the drugs used to treat ADHD. In the midst of all this research, I got to learn firsthand about ADHD through the diagnosis of two close family members. Once I felt like I really was an expert on strategies for ADHD, I wrote a seminar called "Succeeding with Students with ADHD." We had standing-room-only crowds of educators all wanting to know what they could do. The more I traveled, the more I learned as I taught. Everyone wanted to share their stories about their experiences with ADHD, either personally or with students.

I had always known about Learning Disorders (LD), because, once again, a close relative was diagnosed with this at a very young age. I had researched this disorder for years. So many students have both ADHD and LD that it naturally followed that LD came to be included in seminars on ADHD.

As I traveled around the country giving seminars on ADHD and LD, teachers started asking about students with anger disorders like oppositional defiant disorder (ODD). I did the same background research and wrote another seminar, "Succeeding with Angry, Defiant, and ODD Students." It, too, was a huge success.

At that time, very few children were diagnosed with PDD—pervasive developmental disorder; however, numbers soon increased for this as well as for bipolar disorder. Bullying also became a problem in schools. Moreover, teachers complained that more and more children were misbehaving. They couldn't sit still, constantly chattered, complained, tattled, and were disruptive. I wrote a new seminar called "How to Handle the Hard-to-Handle Student." It incorporated ADHD, PDD, anger, defiance, ODD, bullying, bipolar disorder, Tourette's syndrome, obsessive compulsive disorder, and other tough classroom issues like disruptive students, tattling, constant chatter in the classroom, and classroom conflicts. Once again, educators flocked to these seminars to learn strategies for handling these students. National associations for teachers asked to have the subject presented at their conferences.

This book is the result of the demand for strategies to handle these hard-to-handle students. The strategies are all designed to help you help students

- Grow from dependence to independence
- Develop the ability to self-regulate whether or not an adult is present
- Learn how to problem solve
- Learn how to handle their emotions appropriately
- Understand how to behave in ways that meet their needs and the needs of the larger community
- Succeed not only in the classroom but also in life

Each chapter begins with an explanation for each disorder or behavioral problem so that you can have a better understanding as well as recognize the symptoms. Many strategies follow the explanation. The reason there are many strategies is because no one strategy works for all learners. Every learner is unique. What works for one student will not necessarily work for another student, and what works for one student at one time may not work later at another time.

There is also no one strategy that works for all teachers. Teachers all have their own teaching styles, and what is comfortable for one teacher may not be comfortable for another. Each classroom is like a box of crayons. Each crayon color has its own unique beauty. Some of the crayons in the box may be shorter, some longer; some may have pointy tips, and some have been used so much that they are rounded. When these crayons are used together, they create a beautiful drawing. Your classroom is the same. Every student is like one of those crayons—unique and special. This book is packed with strategies to help you open up that crayon box and create your classroom, to unite your class into a "we" instead of a "me."

I sincerely hope you will find this book as valuable as the thousands of people who have taken the training on which it is based.

Acknowledgments

There are so many people who helped me in some way with the writing of this book. This book would not be written if it were not for my friendship with Rick Curwin, another author. Through the years, we have shared many stories of our experiences in the classroom and in speaking to audiences of teachers and parents. One of our shared experiences was Rick introducing me to the people at Corwin Press. I am constantly amazed by the enthusiastic support of the wonderful team at Corwin Press, especially Allyson Sharpe and David Gray, whose enthusiasm for their own work and kind follow-ups have been a constant source of encouragement. Also at Corwin Press, my editor for this book, Jessica Allan, has gently guided me through the writing process. Thank you so much. You have helped make it fun for me to write this book.

I am so grateful to all of the students who have taught me so much. While writing this book, I had the opportunity to see some of the students who are now adults, to speak to them, and to hear what they did with their lives. You inspired me to learn all I could so I could help you, and watching you all succeed has been a gift in my life.

The other great gift in my life has been my own children and grandchildren. I am so blessed to have you all: Marty, Carol, Ciara, Tobi, Sean, Beth, and Gary. Your love fills my heart, mind, and soul.

Thank you to my friend and mentor, Connie, and to my other dear friends. You all are a tremendous support in my life and I am so grateful.

PUBLISHER'S ACKNOWLEDGMENTS

Corwin Press wishes to acknowledge the following peer reviewers for their editorial insight and guidance:

Angela Clinton
3rd/4th Grade Teacher
George T. Daniel Elementary
Kent, WA

Wendy Keen
Education Services Coordinator
Children's Collaborative CPC
Lowell, MA

Jean Kueker
Professor Emeritus of Education, Our Lady of the Lake University
President, Learning Disabilities of Texas
Chairman, Early Childhood Committee for the Learning Disabilities
    Association of America
Burton, TX

Leslie Standerfer
Principal
Estrella Foothills High School
Goodyear, AZ

About the Author

 **Maryln Appelbaum** is well known internationally as an authority on children, education, and families. She has master's degrees in both psychology and education and has completed her doctoral studies in both fields. Maryln worked as a teacher, an administrator, and a therapist and has been an educational consultant throughout the United States. She has written more than 30 how-to books geared toward educators and parents. Maryln has been interviewed on television and radio talk shows and has been quoted in newspapers, including *USA Today*.

She owns a seminar training company, Appelbaum Training Institute, with her son, Marty Appelbaum, and they and their speakers train educators all over the world.

Maryln's influence is felt daily all over the world with her thoughts for the day that go out to thousands of educators via e-mail. Her strategies have been successfully implemented in schools around the world. Not a day goes by that someone does not contact her at the Appelbaum Training Institute to thank her. Those thank yous come from teachers, administrators, parents, and students whose lives have been shaped by Maryln.

Her books and her talks are strategy-based. She does not believe in a "one-size-fits-all" solution and instead provides multiple strategies to reflect the diversity that exists in both learners and teachers. She believes there is a way to help every child succeed. She is enthusiastic, dynamic, dedicated, and caring; a one-of-a-kind difference maker for the world.

How to Handle Students With ADHD

1

ADHD is a "hidden disability."
—Maryln Appelbaum

The first step in working with students with attention-deficit/hyperactivity disorder (ADHD) is to understand that this is a real disability. You can't see it as easily as when you see someone wearing a pair of glasses, using a hearing aid, or sitting in a wheelchair; however, it is still very real. It is a disorder that is often invisible, buried beneath what appears to be misbehavior, sloppiness, laziness, and even stubbornness. I call it the hidden disability.

ADHD has been around a long time. Over one hundred years ago, the medical community focused attention on a combination of deficits in attention, learning, motor skills, and motivation (Gillberg, 2003). The name for this combination of deficits changed over the years, and today it has come to be called ADHD. It is the most common mental disorder of childhood (Stolzer, 2007) and affects 7.5 percent of school-age children (Fine, 2002) in the United States. The ADHD diagnosis accounts for 50 percent of the children in child psychiatry clinics in America (Leslie, Weckerly, Plemmons, Landsyerk, & Eastman, 2004). It is a very real disorder.

When I think of an executive, I think of someone who is in charge of a large company. That person performs many functions to organize employees and ensure that the company operates smoothly. The brain also has executive functions—functions to ensure that operations are organized. There are several executive functions that may be affected in children with ADHD (Stearns, Dunham, McIntosh, & Dean, 2004).

A very important executive function is nonverbal memory. This is the child's ability to keep representations—pictures of events—in the mind. These pictures then become part of children's memories. These pictures are very important because they help children see what will happen if they engage in an action. Students with ADHD often have a deficit with this executive function, and because they cannot see what will happen, they act impulsively.

Another very important executive function is working memory (Biederman et al., 2000, as cited by Stearns et al., 2004). Working memory stores and manipulates information to do tasks. Students need working memory to not only do their schoolwork, but also to remember the rules of behavior and problem solving. When students have a deficit in working memory, they do not remember to stop engaging in inappropriate behaviors. That is why students with ADHD often engage in the same inappropriate behaviors repeatedly, even though they have experienced consequences. Teachers have said to me, "I don't understand. They get in trouble every time. Why do they just keep doing it?" It is because it is not in their working memory.

Students with ADHD generally have problems following rules. This is because of another deficit in executive function—self-regulation. Self-regulation is important because this is the function that gives students the self-discipline they need to set goals and work toward those goals. They need this so they can sustain attention to tasks, even when they are disinterested, bored, or tired. When this function is operating, they learn to set a plan in motion, and they follow through until it is finished. They do not need anyone to look over their shoulders to ensure they are moving toward their goals.

All of these functions are internal. You cannot see these functions, so it is easy to forget they are there. Instead, you may think, "Petey is lazy." "He hates following rules." "He never follows through." "It's in one ear, and out the other." "He loses everything." "I never know what he will do next."

A huge problem is that students start believing they are not as good as their peers. I met Sherry, an adult with ADHD, while I was giving seminars on ADHD. Sherry told me that she always felt different from other children. She never fit in with her peers, and she felt like she never could get anything right. She compared herself to her older sister who did not have ADHD. Sadly, her parents also compared her to her sister, and Sherry came up short! No one knew she had ADHD. Everyone, both at school and at home, thought she was deliberately not following through when asked to do something. They thought she was lazy and stubborn and not very smart. Actually, Sherry had an above-average IQ, but it was not readily seen because of her lack of follow-through on assignments and tasks.

Unfortunately, no one diagnosed her until late into adulthood. By then, her self-esteem had been severely affected.

There are ways to help students with ADHD (Brown, Ilderton, Taylor, & Lock, 2001). One method is the medical model of giving them medication, usually a stimulant. Medicating children does not always solve the problem. There are children who need medication but do not get it, and other children who take medication but do not need it. There are also students who get medication, but the dose may not be appropriate. Teachers speak repeatedly of overmedicated students acting like "zombies."

I will never forget one man who spoke to me about medication. I was in a small town in New Mexico. I had just completed a morning session for a large group of parents of students with ADHD. I was taking a break, and then I was going to do the same session for teachers. As I stood near my computer sorting through my PowerPoint presentation for the next session, a tall, slim, fair-haired man came up to me. He introduced himself to me as a dad whose son had been diagnosed the year before with ADHD. He told me that he had been very upset with the doctor when his son was placed on Ritalin because he did not want his son medicated. His ex-wife had custody, so it was her decision. But then something amazing happened; his son began to act totally differently. He could focus. His grades dramatically improved. The dad was very impressed, and it made him start thinking about himself. He had had problems his whole life both in learning and in relationships. He decided to go to his son's doctor to see if he, too, had ADHD. The doctor did a full workup, diagnosed him with ADHD, and put him on Ritalin. This dad had a look of amazement on his face as he told me that up to the day he started taking Ritalin, he had never read a book from cover to cover. Once he started taking Ritalin, he got a library card and started reading book after book. He could focus. He could concentrate. I can still picture the look of awe on his face as he shared his story of how medication had helped him.

The American Psychiatric Association (2000) identifies several types of ADHD. All types have in common a chronic and persistent pattern of inattention, hyperactivity, and impulsivity.

ADHD INATTENTIVE TYPE

Students with this type of ADHD have many symptoms of being inattentive. (See Figure 1.1) One of the key symptoms is that they have trouble listening and following directions and have difficulty focusing and sustaining attention. They may start out listening to what the teacher is saying, but their minds drift off to other topics. This happens all the time, not only when in class. It can happen when students are reading a book or listening to a friend. Their minds wander, and they are easily distracted. The distraction can be auditory like an airplane flying outside, raindrops on the window, or even air conditioning or heating vents. It can be visual like a fancy bulletin board at the front of the room or even something about the teacher's appearance.

Gardner was a third grader with ADHD Inattentive Type. He was a quiet, shy boy, the type of child who could easily fall through the cracks. He did not misbehave or dress in any unusual way. His teacher, Mrs. Jenkins, was a first-year teacher. She put most of her attention on students who were misbehaving. One day, however, Mrs. Jenkins did notice Gardner. He was looking at her in a peculiar manner instead of responding to instructions about group work the students were to begin. She walked over to him and asked if something was wrong. He said, "Mrs. Jenkins, I'm sorry. I couldn't hear you talking because I was watching your hands—your red nail polish." He had become completely distracted by her nail polish. From that day on, Mrs. Jenkins never wore bright nail polish.

Because of this inattentiveness, students may start a task and not finish it. Their schoolwork is often inconsistent. Some days they may be able to focus better than others. On the days that they can't focus as well, they may look "spacey." Their attention just wanders from object to object and situation to situation. They may forget from moment to moment what they were doing.

Students with ADHD Inattentive Type have a tendency to procrastinate. They wait until the last possible minute to do an assignment. Waiting until the last minute actually stimulates the brain. When they feel rushed, they feel stimulated to focus and get the job done. It's their way of attending to a task. Of course, sometimes, the task doesn't get done at all because the student totally forgets about it. This difficulty completing tasks affects their grades adversely (Reiter, 2004).

While students with ADHD generally have difficulty focusing, there are times when they can hyper-focus on a task and tune out everything and everyone else. A great example of this is when students use the computer or watch television. Everything is tuned out for hours at a time. When a project is interesting at school, this same hyper-focusing characteristic can help students work for hours at a time.

Another characteristic of inattentive students is that they are often disorganized. They may lose or forget their belongings. These are the students who come to school without homework and truly did forget it or misplace it. They cannot find their belongings like paper, pencils, or books. Their desks and lockers may be total disasters with papers scattered everywhere and items upside down. All of this contributes to these children feeling like, "I can't get anything right. Why even try?" Once this type of learned helplessness occurs, it will be even harder to help students succeed (Valas, 2001). This child can be helped. It simply takes new tools.

Strategies for Succeeding With Students With ADHD Inattentive Type

The Edutainer

An edutainer is a word that I made up many years ago. An edutainer is both an educator and an entertainer. You have to do this to hold the attention of students. Be so engaging that students want to listen to you as much as they want to watch their favorite television show or play a video game. There was a time when children came to school, and even if they had ADHD, they sat still and listened as best as they could. They had

Figure 1.1 Checklist of Behavioral Characteristics of ADHD Inattentive Type

☐ Difficulty listening

☐ Difficulty attending to tasks

☐ Difficulty focusing

☐ Easily distracted

☐ Procrastinates

☐ Problems concentrating

☐ Inconsistent performance in school work

☐ Disorganized

☐ Loses belongings

☐ Cluttered desk and room

☐ Poor study skills

☐ Forgetful

☐ Problems working independently

that old fashioned R-word, "respect." They learned at home that when they came to school, they had better pay attention. That is generally not the case anymore. Instead, students come to school with an entirely different attitude: "Entertain me." They are used to watching television, playing video games, seeing entertainment. Now, as part of educating, teachers have to entertain, too. That is what it means to be an edutainer.

At seminars I show an awesome video clip that illustrates this point. A man is standing on a stage and starts to play his trombone. He hooks his audience's attention immediately by swinging his hips and rolling around on stage as he plays the trombone. He has zest; he has spirit. Soon, the audience members stand up and start swinging to the beat. He has captivated their attention. Everyone in my own audience laughs as they see this, and some get up and start swinging around just from watching it. He is an edutainer.

Brain research shows that there are different ways to engage the brain (Jenson, 2000). One fun way is to do something novel. For example, the first time I got on a plane after 9/11, I was feeling frightened. Usually, flight attendants give a tedious speech about seatbelts and oxygen masks right before the planes take off, and typically, passengers tune it out because they have heard it so many times before. This time, when many passengers were uneasy, the flight attendant greeted us all with a smile and instead of droning on, she sang the safety information. She deliberately made funny voice inflections as she sang. She was an edutainer and held our attention totally. This is a technique you can use. Laugh and have fun. Burst into song unexpectedly. Edutain and help all students in your class focus and pay attention.

Eliminating Distractions

Because students with ADHD are so easily distracted, seating is crucial (Carroll et al., 2006). Noises can be extremely distracting. If they sit near an air conditioning or heating vent, they may find it very difficult to concentrate, listening to the noise of the air from the vent rather than you. If they sit near the door, they can hear the sounds from the hallway. It's not only sounds that are distracting, but also sights. Students sitting near a window will be easily distracted by the sights outside the window. If students with ADHD are sitting near the back of the room, all of the students in front of them will distract them. They will notice what the other children are wearing, what they are doing, and how they are sitting, instead of putting their attention on you.

Your clothing makes a difference. Even scents you wear can be distracting. Strong perfume or aftershave may distract students. Some students have said that long earrings worn by teachers distracted them because they swung around while the teacher spoke. Others have reported that they were distracted by the walls behind the teacher. There were all kinds of posters, writing, and messages on those walls that held their attention more than the teacher did. Students with ADHD notice everything (Carroll). Their attention can be caught by sights and sounds you take for granted. If a student starts showing symptoms of inattentiveness, something as simple as changing the student's seat can totally change the student's behavior.

Headphones or ear plugs are another way of blocking out distractions. These are especially beneficial for students who are extremely sensitive to sounds.

Private Offices. An effective device to maintain attention is to give students "private offices." Open two manila file folders side by side. Slide one of the folders partially into the other folder so that the folders overlap, creating three "walls." The "private office" can stand up on a desk. Have students individualize the offices by decorating the outsides of the folders, but the insides remain blank. When students need to concentrate on their work, they get out their "offices" and work at their seats in privacy.

Staying on Task

It can be very difficult for students with ADHD to stay on task. There are several ways you can help them (Parker, 2005). One way is for you to use sticky notes as reminders on their worksheets or homework. Another way is for them to write their own reminders. Have them make a list of all the things they need to remember. They then write each reminder on separate sticky notes. Now they are ready to take the sticky notes and pop them on the pages of their assignments.

Erasable Highlighters. Students enjoy working with erasable highlighters, and the highlighters help them stay on task. Students highlight the information they need to remember. Later, they can erase what they wrote. Erasable highlighters can be found at most office supply stores. Different colors can be used for different reminders. For example, when studying parts of speech, nouns can be highlighted using yellow and verbs highlighted with pink.

Underlining. If you don't want to use erasable highlighters, teach students to put a line under all completed work. They learn that anything without a line underneath it still needs to be finished. This is another way of helping them to stay on task.

Visual Task Cards. List the items students need to do on a sheet of paper. Call it a visual task card. As students complete each item, they check it off. This is an effective strategy that can also be shared with families. Some parents report great success when they put task cards on the refrigerator. Every time children get something from the refrigerator, they are reminded of tasks that still need to be completed.

Proximity Control. Proximity control is an excellent method for helping all students, not just those with ADHD, stay on task (Gunter & Shores, 1995). When you see a student talking to other students or not doing an assignment, walk over to the student's desk. Touch the desk, smile at the student, and point to the work or put your finger on your mouth to indicate it is time to "shhh." This is an effective strategy for nipping problems in the bud before they develop into classroom management issues.

Dividing Work. Students with ADHD often become so overwhelmed when they look at a paper filled with assignments that they may freeze before they even get started. Mrs. Sloan had that problem with Daren. She solved this problem by taking a blue file folder and cutting the front flap of the folder into three horizontal equal parts. She numbered the parts one through three from top to bottom. She then put the assignment sheet inside the folder. She told Daren to first open up section one, the top section, and do the problems. When he was finished, he closed the top section. He then opened up section two, the middle section, and worked those problems. When he finished that section, he closed it and opened section three, the bottom section, and worked those problems. When he finished section three, he opened up the top two sections to make sure that he had finished the entire sheet. This was a great way for him to do his classwork without feeling overwhelmed.

Organizing Tools

One of the characteristics of students with ADHD Inattentive Type is disorganization. The more organized students are, the more effective their work will be. Look at the areas of disorganization and then focus on finding strategies to help students succeed, like color coding and labeling.

Color Coding. Color coding is an effective strategy to help students with ADHD stay organized and keep track of their work (Brown et al., 2001). Use different colors for different subjects. For example, the math book has a red paper book cover, a red folder to hold all math papers, and little red dots on the backs of all math equipment, which is stored on shelves with red tape on the edges. Other subject areas have other colors; you can use different colors like red for math, blue for language, yellow for social studies, and green for science. Color coding not only helps students stay more organized, but it also serves as a great reminder of where to put things when finished using them.

Label. Have lockers that are clearly labeled. Put a picture at the top of the locker showing where everything goes. This serves as a visual reminder every time students put anything in their lockers.

Use the same technique for desks. Have a photo inside the desk lid showing where everything needs to go. Have a set time each day in which students do their daily desk checks to make sure everything is in the correct place. It is important that this is done daily because it doesn't take long for a mess to accumulate inside desks.

Names on Work. Students with ADHD often forget to put their names on their papers. I have used several strategies very effectively to help them remember. One way is to highlight papers ahead of time with yellow highlighter in the area on the page for the student's name. At the beginning of each class period, have the students write their names where the yellow highlighter is marked on their sheets.

I have another fun method for having students write their names, called "pencils in the air." When it is time for students to do their assignments, I have them get out their sheets of paper, and we play a "Simon Says" type of game. They love games. They have to do everything that I tell them to do. I give them a bunch of silly instructions like "Touch your nose," and then I tell them, "Pencils in the air." The students all hold up their pencils. The next instruction is "Pencils down on the top of the paper." This is followed by, "Write your names on the paper." After that, there are usually some more fun instructions like having students smile at someone sitting next to them, putting their hands on top of their desks, clapping their hands, and even saying, "I love this assignment." Students laugh and have fun. Anxiety is reduced, and names are on the papers.

Peer Support

Assign students with ADHD who are forgetful a "remember partner." The remember partner is a student who is very organized and enjoys being a helper (Parker, 2005). The remember partner's job is to remind the student of important assignments and lessons. Choose the remember partner carefully because it is important that the two students are compatible.

Pocket Folders

Students often forget or become confused about bringing work back to school after they have finished it at home. They sometimes bring back assignment sheets over and over again that they no longer need, sheets that really can stay home. An easy organizing strategy to help students with this situation is to use different-colored folders for each subject area. Each folder needs to have two pockets when opened, one on the left and one on the right. Mark the pocket on the left to say, "Left at home." This means that papers in this pocket go home and stay home. Mark the pocket on the right, "Right back to school." This means that students are to complete those pages in that pocket and return them to school.

Clipboard

If there is anything really important that you want parents to see, attach it to a clipboard. It's difficult for students to forget or lose a big, hard clipboard.

Launching Pad

Students often forget to bring pencils, pens, homework assignments, and sometimes even their lunch. Suggest to parents to create a "launching pad" area at home. It can be a chair or a small table. The student puts homework, special shoes, a sweater, pencils, pens, books, and anything else that needs to be brought to school on the launching pad. These items are with the student's backpack but not in the backpack. Things that go into the backpack frequently get lost. The last thing the student does before going to school is to place every object on the launching pad into the backpack. Ideally, the backpacks can be color coded with one bag for morning classes and another for afternoon classes.

ADHD HYPERACTIVE-IMPULSIVE TYPE

Just as the word hyperactive implies, students with this form of ADHD are very active and need to move around (Frank, 2001). They are often restless and cannot sit still for long periods of time. They are in constant motion. These are the students who tap their pencils, get up from their seats to roam around the room, and sometimes even fall out of their chairs. When they are sitting, they may be moving their hands, tapping their fingers, or swinging their legs back and forth. Their mouths are in motion too, talking, blurting out inappropriately, or chewing on a pencil or other object.

They are often frustrated, and may become angry at others and say things they do not mean. Sometimes, they don't even remember what it is they said that got someone upset. They just said what popped into their minds without thinking through the ramifications. This causes hurt feelings and sometimes failed relationships.

While it is easy to become upset with these children, it's important to remember that they do have a disorder. It is as real as diabetes. Underneath all the hyperactivity and impulsive behavior may be a very lonely child. See Figure 1.2 below.

Figure 1.2 Checklist of Behavioral Characteristics of ADHD Hyperactive-Impulsive Type

☐ High activity level

☐ Appears to be in constant motion

☐ Plays with objects

☐ Puts objects in mouth

☐ Talks excessively

☐ Difficulty waiting for turn

☐ Roams around classroom

☐ Great difficulty staying in seat

☐ Often fidgets with hands or feet

☐ Impulsive and lacks self-control

☐ Blurts out verbally

☐ Engages in impulsive behaviors

☐ Gets in trouble frequently

☐ Difficulty in personal relationships

☐ Often interrupts others

☐ Difficulty with transitions

☐ Easily frustrated

Strategies for Succeeding With Students With ADHD Hyperactive-Impulsive Type

The strategies you will be learning in this section are all designed to provide appropriate ways for students to move within the classroom. They need to move. It helps them concentrate and stay focused. It is not something that they *want* to do, but rather something that they *have* to do.

Mouse Pad

Students who are hyperactive often fidget with their hands. They often tap their fingers, pens, or pencils loudly on their desks. Give these students something else to tap—something that does not make noise. A computer mouse pad is perfect. When students feel like tapping their fingers or pencils, they tap onto the mouse pad, and no one is disturbed. Students get to tap, and the classroom gets to be quieter.

Kenzie was in constant trouble for making too much noise in the classroom from kindergarten through fourth grade. He couldn't sit still; he was in constant motion. He continually tapped his pencil or pen on the desk. It was so loud that it distracted the entire class. In the fifth grade, everything changed for Kenzie. His teacher, Ms. Saven, taught him a new strategy. She told him it was OK with her if he tapped his pencil or pen. She gave him a computer mouse pad and told him that anytime he felt like tapping, he was to tap the pen or pencil on the mouse pad. He continued to tap, but now he was not disturbing anyone. He had learned an appropriate behavior to substitute for the inappropriate behavior. This method, along with others in this section, helped Kenzie to thrive in his classroom and as he progressed into middle school. He had learned new behaviors to replace the old, inappropriate behaviors.

Energy Ball

You will need a stress ball for this strategy. Call it an "energy ball." Students take their excess energy and use it to squeeze the ball. They squeeze and squeeze the ball until they feel better and are able to keep their hands and bodies still. In one classroom that used this technique successfully, quiet, shy Megan came up to her teacher one day with a question. She said, "Mrs. Patterson, if the other kids can put their energy into the ball, can I use it to get some energy? I'm really tired today because I couldn't fall asleep last night." Mrs. Patterson said, "Sure," and Megan squeezed it and squeezed it until she felt better!

Stress Bucket

Some teachers have a "stress bucket" filled with different-shaped stress balls. They add to the bucket cut-up squares of soft fabric like velvet and even small squares of cut-up shag carpeting. This is effective because children like to squeeze different textures.

Velcro

There are some students who may become embarrassed when classmates see them holding a stress object in their hands. Place a small square of Velcro under these students' desks. When students feel like moving their hands, they can rub the Velcro.

Doodle Pad

In their need for movement, some students doodle all over their assignments. By the time the assignments are turned in, they are unreadable. Give these students a doodle pad, a separate pad of paper that students can doodle on so assignments are turned in clean and easy to read.

Twist Bracelets

Some students who move their hands excessively develop a habit of twisting and pulling on their hair, and they actually can pull their hair out from their scalp. Teach them a different strategy for their hands when they feel like twisting something by giving them a small rope bracelet. Whenever they feel like twisting their hair, they twist the bracelet instead. Be careful that students do not twist the bracelet so strongly that they harm their wrists. If you see this happening, suggest that they hold and twist the bracelet rather than wear it.

Errands

It's readily apparent which students need to move their entire bodies. They fidget and sometimes even fall out of their seats. They need strategies that will allow them to move their legs without disrupting the class. One effective strategy is to give these students errands within the classroom. They can empty the trash, help clean shelves, or carry something from one end of the room to the other.

Empty Desk

When you have students who need to move their entire bodies, use the empty desk strategy. Have an empty desk up at the front of the room.

When students need to move, they move quietly to the other desk without touching anyone or talking. There are some students who go back and forth between the two desks every 10–15 minutes. As long as students do it quietly without disrupting the class, this is allowable.

Standing Room Only

Another effective strategy for students who cannot sit still is to have the student's desk in an area of the room that won't be disruptive to the class. Use colored masking tape to mark a large square around the student's desk. Within this "standing room only" area, the student is free to sit or stand or move about quietly without disrupting the class.

BOTH ADHD INATTENTIVE AND ADHD HYPERACTIVE-IMPULSIVE TYPES

Strategies for Succeeding With Students With ADHD Inattentive Type and Students With ADHD Hyperactive-Impulsive Type

Deadlines

Students with ADHD generally have no innate concept of time. They only see *now*, not the future and not the past. They generally tend to overestimate or underestimate how long it will take to complete specific tasks. They are task oriented rather than time structured. If interested in a task, students start it and work on it until it is finished or until they have collapsed from exhaustion. However, if the task is not interesting or if there is no deadline pressure, students will typically avoid beginning the task at all.

The key is to make each task interesting and relevant. Make assignments come alive so that students are excited. The more relevant it is, the more they will want to do it.

Each day, count down to the due date of an important assignment so that the deadline remains in students' minds. Have the date due written on the board so that they have the visual assist as well as the auditory one.

Self-Monitoring

Students need to learn how to work independently. Teach them self-monitoring skills (Harris, Friedlander, Saddler, Frizzelle, & Graham, 2005). Show them how to break assignments into smaller chunks. Teach them to set a time that each chunk of work will be completed. Students monitor themselves to ensure that they have completed the work in the designated time period.

A stopwatch or timer is an effective way to help students self-monitor. Students set the timer for the time they are scheduled to work on a task. They work hard to ensure that what they are doing is completed before the time on the timer or stopwatch runs out.

Homework Checklist

Homework checklists are tools for families and schools to ensure that students complete their homework. Have a special sheet of paper (see Figure 1.3) to record the homework that is due for each subject under the appropriate day of the week. Students take the checklist home nightly. Students do the homework in each subject, and parents initial the checklist, confirming that the homework has been completed. Students then put their homework and the homework checklist on the launching pad so they remember to bring it back to school the next day.

Clear Directions

I have found that students with ADHD often do not follow directions because they do not fully understand them. The good news is that there are ways to give them directions so that they do understand (Frank, 2001). Give only one direction at a time, and demonstrate what you want them to do. Students need that visual explanation. Once you have demonstrated, have them take a turn rehearsing the directions. Keep directions brief. Use words that are easy for them to understand. Here's an example of clear directions: "I have a really fun assignment for you to do in class today. Here's how you will do it. Everyone take out a sheet of paper." Wait until they all have paper out. "Write your name right here." Hold up paper and show them where to write their names. "Put numbers one through five on the paper right here like this one on the overhead." Show them a paper on an overhead that is numbered one through five. Walk around the room as they are writing the numbers to be sure they understand.

Traffic Light Signals

Most students are embarrassed to say that they do not understand something being taught or cannot figure out how to work a problem. To constantly monitor whether your class understands, make traffic light signals for each of your students. Take a white sheet of paper and fold it

Figure 1.3 Homework Checklist

Homework

Student's Name _____ Week of _____

Subject	Monday	Tuesday	Wednesday	Thursday	Friday
Parent's Initials					

vertically into three equal sections. On each section, draw a huge circle. Fill in the circle on the top section with green to make the "green light." Fill in the middle circle with yellow for the "yellow light." Fill in the bottom circle with red to be the "red light." Fold the paper back into three equal parts so it can stand up with one side facing the front of the classroom. Pass out the traffic light signals to your students to place on their desks. When students fully understand the task or what is being learned, they have the "green light" face the front of the room. When they are not quite sure, they set the traffic light on "yellow" to face the front of the classroom. When they have no idea what they are supposed to be doing or learning, they have the "red light" face the front of the classroom. It's an effective way of continually assessing students so you know who needs your help.

Frequent Support and Encouragement

Your smile is worth riches to students who struggle. Affirm students when they act appropriately (Bowman, Carr, Cooper, Miles, & Toner, 1998). Let them know that you believe in them. Your positive words and comments can make a huge difference in the lives of your children. You just never know the difference you make. Kasinda was a really tough student I had early in my teaching career. She was taller than any other student in my class, very slim, with a long, dark ponytail and huge, hardened eyes. She had a hard time concentrating, forgot to do her assignments, and would retreat into her own world. She was angry often, talked back when asked to do anything, and treated me and all the other students with disrespect. I checked into her background and learned that her dad had left before she was born, and her mom had left a few years later. She was being raised by an elderly grandmother who was exhausted. The grandmother felt like a failure because of what had happened with her daughter and now had just given up on Kasinda.

I resolved that I would help Kasinda. I set aside a special time each day to meet with her alone for five minutes. I told her that I wanted to get to know her and mostly listened as she talked. The early sessions were frequently for her to vent anger. She talked about how she hated her mother, her dad, and even her grandmother. Slowly, she began to trust me. She said she had no friends and told me that she really didn't know how to get friends. I asked her if she would like me to pair her up with a "learning buddy." She thought about that for nearly a week before she told me to go ahead. I did, and soon she and her learning buddy became friends. It was amazing to watch Kasinda that school year, as I met with her daily. Her eyes became brighter, and she went from an unhappy, sullen child to becoming a happier child. What a joy!

One day, many years later, I was leading a seminar, and a tall, attractive woman came up to me and introduced herself. It was Kasinda! She had on her great smile. She was now a teacher and loved her work. She thanked me for taking the time to be there for her when she really needed it and she said that she became a teacher so she could do the same thing for other children. You just never know the difference that you make each day in the lives of your students.

How to Handle Students With Learning Disabilities

2

Today's child is tomorrow's future.
—Maryln Appelbaum

This topic has very a special meaning for me because two close family members were both labeled with learning disabilities (LD). They are both adults now, and while they had many struggles they had to overcome as children, they are now both successful in their lives. I share this story at the beginning of this chapter because, even though having LD can be devastating, there is hope.

Individuals with LD have a neurological impairment that mixes up signals between the brain and the senses (Winebrenner, 2006). Students with LD may have an average or above-average intelligence. They can see and hear, but they do it differently. They have a neurological impairment in perception, conceptualization, language, memory, attention, or motor control. LD affects approximately five percent of students (American Psychiatric Association, 2000).

Here is an exercise that I use at the beginning of every seminar in which I teach about LD. I have the audience members pair up and say the alphabet backwards. Then I have them do it again, but with a twist. They have to say the alphabet backwards, and between each letter, they must insert the name of a city, country, or state that does not begin with those two letters (e.g., "Z, California, Y").

Audience members all flounder, grin sheepishly, and say that this task is very difficult. I then explain that this is how learning feels for students with LD. Learning something new is this difficult and frustrating for students with LD.

Students hear the sounds, but their brains may mix up the signals. The same is true for what they see. For example, the sentence, "The train goes fast" may look to students with LD like, "The rain goes fast." They may omit just one letter, totally changing the context. They may omit an entire word, and the sentence could read, "The goes fast." Words may be blurred so that they are hard to read. Every time they read the same sentence or word, it can change again.

Students with LD may also have problems with long-term memory. They may struggle to learn a concept like a math fact and then later forget it. It is erased to the point that it does not seem like it was ever learned. If all of this appears frustrating to teachers, it is even more frustrating for students. Students struggle with feeling like they are dumb, even though they are actually bright. They often suffer from low self-esteem because of feeling like failures in school. Nearly 40 percent of students with LD drop out of school (American Psychiatric Association, 2000). They need strategies to help them feel successful and people to believe in them.

STRATEGIES FOR SUCCEEDING WITH STUDENTS WITH LD

You can help students with LD. The first step is to recognize that these students are not lazy or unmotivated. They have a real disability. They may become unmotivated if they continue to fail. Your task is to help keep them motivated by finding strategies that work.

Strategies for ADHD

Many of the strategies suggested in the previous chapter apply to students with LD. They, too, benefit from all of the organizational strategies as well as other strategies. Review the strategies for ADHD and use them with your students who have LD.

Note Taker

When students with LD take notes, they often can't read their own writing, misspell words, leave out words, and have very little to show for their efforts. It is then difficult for them to use those notes to study for tests. Assign someone who takes good class notes to take notes for the other student. Give the note taker carbonless paper and put an extra sheet of paper underneath the page, so that whenever they write, they are automatically making two pages. Assign students who you know like helping others as note takers. Make sure that students with LD are not embarrassed by having someone else take notes. If they are embarrassed, have the notes taken anonymously so that note takers do not know who will be receiving the notes.

Testing

Allow students who struggle with completing tests under a timetable to take tests in a separate room or at a different time. Have someone read the test questions to the student. This can dramatically improve test scores because now the student with LD knows exactly what is being asked. The student sees the visual test and hears the test questions so that both auditory and visual modes of learning are accommodated.

Reading Strategies

Because reading is often a real problem with students with LD, it is important to have a bag of tricks to help students succeed.

Reading Aloud

Have students read aloud to a study buddy. This is preferable to students making mistakes while reading silently and not even knowing they are making the mistakes. Reading aloud to a study buddy also helps them to stay focused and avoid distractions.

Tracing With Fingers or Highlighter

Students with LD often lose their place as they read. There are strategies you can use to help them keep their place. Erasable highlighters can be found in office supply stores. Still another way of highlighting without an actual highlighter is to teach students to trace words with their fingers as they read. This helps them keep their place on the page.

Word Windows

Use word windows, which can typically be purchased inexpensively at teacher supply stores, to help students stay focused. They are small, laminated, rectangular sheets that fit on a regular page in a book or in a notebook. A transparent opening in the center allows students to see only one line on the page to help them focus on the passage they are reading. This transparent opening typically is yellow or blue, a color that serves as a highlighter to help students keep their place as they read.

Colored Transparencies

One simple correction that helps many students read better is placing colored transparent sheets of paper over students' reading material. Suddenly, words that were blurred and jumbled on white paper become clearer and easier to read. Different students need different colors of transparent sheets. Inexpensive sheets are often available at a scrapbooking store, and you can purchase a variety of colors to determine which colors work best for students.

Show the different colors to students with LD who have problems reading. Place them on top of pages of white paper with black print. Ask the students to tell you which colors work best. Many students choose yellow, but other students may choose another color. Once you know the color that helps the child, you can recommend that parents buy glasses with lenses in that color. Transparent sheets may become blurry with hand and fingerprints. Lenses in the glasses can be more easily cleaned.

Audio Assists

Whenever possible, provide verbal assists. Audio tapes of books and even instructions can help students. A study buddy who reads to the student is another audio assist. Ideally, combine both the visual with the auditory assist. Students follow along in their texts visually as they hear the words read out loud.

E-Books and Recorded Books

Some students have a difficult time reading print, yet they do better with e-books. Other students do well listening to recorded books. Discover the way each of your students learns best, and you will have gone a long way to helping them succeed.

Phonemic Awareness and Phonics Activities

Do phonemic awareness lessons and phonics activities with students at all levels. This is an area of weakness for many students with LD. The more they practice, the better they generally can perform.

Spelling Strategies

If reading does not come naturally, neither does spelling. Students with LD need assistance to be more successful at spelling.

Repeat Words

Have students slowly repeat words as they spell. This helps them to identify the connections between sounds and letters. Have them repeat the word several times to themselves until they can hear individual sounds.

First Three Letters

Teach students to look at the first three letters of a word before they say the word. They often only look at the first letter and guess at the word. This simple little trick teaches them to look more closely at the word.

Tactfulness

Be tactful. When students make an error, instead of immediately correcting them, offer corrections in a more positive manner. Instead of saying, "That's wrong, Jeff," say, "Let me show you another way to read this." These are students who easily feel like failures. The more they feel like they cannot succeed, the more they really cannot succeed. Your words can help ease the discomfort of making a mistake. Your voice tone is as important as your words. When they hear "I believe in you—you can do this," in your voice, it helps them to believe in themselves, too.

Fun and Interesting Books

Have you ever read a book that you just could not put down? You read and read and read, putting off doing other things. The book had you totally hooked. Finding a fascinating book is important for students with LD during independent reading time. It can be a huge chore for them to read something that is not interesting. Find out what interests them, and offer them books and articles to read in their area of interest.

Michael was one of my students with LD. He hated reading. He struggled with his schoolwork and often did not finish assignments. I discovered that he was interested in fish. He had a fish tank at home and knew the names of and interesting details about each of the fish. The first time I gave him a book to read about aquariums, he read it quickly. I used that book as a jump start to get him engaged in other topics the class was studying. When we had a geography lesson about Alaska, I had him research what types of fish were native to Alaska. You can use this strategy with your students; find their hooks, their subjects of interest, and build on them.

Penmanship

Students with LD often have trouble with penmanship. They may make reversals and have difficulty with handwriting.

Visual Strip

Students often reverse letters or numerals. One effective strategy is to attach a visual strip to the student's desk so there is a model for the letters or numbers that give the student trouble. The students look at the letters on the visual strip and copy them.

Hidden Answers

There may be another reason for the reversals. I had a student in my school named Cory. He was a good-natured, short, and chubby kindergartner. Cory's dad was the president of a large bank and was used to telling people what to do and how to do it. He was frustrated with Cory's reversals, especially with the letters *b* and *d*. I met with Cory's father at a teacher conference. He told me he had practiced and practiced with Cory, but Cory still kept making reversals. He said that Cory even used to write with his left hand and that it took him months to get Cory to use his right hand. He was pleased that Cory was finally using his right hand after months of nagging.

The next day, I decided to do an experiment with Cory. I gave him a sheet of paper and told him to write some words that had the letters *b* and *d* sprinkled throughout. I told him that this time, I wanted him to write with his left hand. At first, he did not want to use his left hand. He told me that his dad told him not to use it. Finally, he agreed for that one time to use his left hand. Cory copied the words perfectly with no reversals at all. I called his dad and told him what happened, and he agreed that from that time on, Cory could use his left hand. Cory never had any further problems with reversals.

Over the course of the years, this reoccurred several times with other students. When it did not work, I provided a model for students on the desk. I also had the letters written on a piece of paper with arrows showing where to start. Students traced the letters over and over again until it became second nature to write the letters correctly.

Prepare the Hand

One of the most important strategies for teaching students to write is to prepare the hand. Look at your hand right now as you are reading this. Pretend to hold a pencil. You are holding together your thumb, forefinger, and middle finger. Those are called "pincer fingers," which are the fingers that grip a pencil or pen. The more you prepare students to use those fingers, the better they will be able to write.

An excellent exercise for the pincer fingers is tonging. You will need two same-sized small soup bowls, a pair of tongs, a sponge cut into small pieces, and a tray that holds all of the items. Fill the bowl on the left with the cut-up pieces of sponge. The bowl on the right is empty. Demonstrate slowly taking the tongs and moving one sponge at a time from the right bowl to the left bowl. When you are finished, turn the tray so that the full bowl is once again on the left. Make sure students always use the tongs from left to right, because you are indirectly training their eyes to go from left to right. That is the way students read a book and write—from left to right.

Once students have mastered tonging using large tongs, replace the tongs with tweezers and smaller objects. Students use the tweezers to move smaller objects from the bowl on the left to a bowl on the right.

The more those pincer fingers are developed, the better students will write. It is similar to developing muscles when going to a gym. Several years ago, my son and daughter-in-law bought me a gym membership for my birthday. When I went to the gym, the trainers started me with very small weights. Gradually, over time, they gave me larger and larger weights. First, I had to learn how to handle the weights, how to hold them, and how to lift them. It is the same with teaching writing. The hand needs to be prepared before students can lift those pencils or pens and begin writing.

Tracing

When students are ready to start writing, have them trace the letter with their fingers. Have them practice making letters on a chalkboard, where the letters can be easily erased. When they have mastered the chalkboard, they are ready to write their letters on a sheet of paper.

Math Strategies

Math is a subject that students with LD may find a struggle. It is important to help students feel successful. Every school has its own math program, so these strategies are meant to help you help your students succeed within the programs you have already implemented.

Making Math Concrete

Learning math involves taking an abstract concept and making it concrete in the minds of students. The best way to teach math is to use manipulatives that students can see, feel, and count. They need to be able to see what different numbers look like. That is why so many students count on their fingers. Those students are actually saying to you, "I learn best when I see, feel, and touch the numbers." The more concretely you teach math, the more easily students will learn.

Counting as a Foundation

You can learn to read without memorizing the alphabet, but it is impossible to do any math operations without knowing how to count. Students need to learn one-to-one correspondence. They have to learn that what they are saying corresponds to objects. Ask them to hand you one of an object. Have them take two objects and place them somewhere. Count whenever possible in your classroom. Count students as they line up. Count desks in the room. Count the days of the week. Count the hands of how many students have pets at home. Have students join you as you count. The more they count, the better prepared they will be for mathematical operations.

Whole Body Math

To teach a number line, have students line up. Tell them they are standing on 0. Have them move one step to the right. Now tell them they are standing on 1. Have them take three more steps to the right. Tell them they are standing on 4. Because they are using their bodies to count, students get this. They see it, feel it, and understand it. The more multisensory experiences you use, the better students can learn (Winebrenner, 2006).

Multiplication Tables

Students often have a tough time learning their multiplication tables, which are the basis for so many more operations. Provide students with a CD of the multiplication tables set to music and have them sing and clap their way through the tables. That is a good way for them to memorize the tables. If you have access to concrete objects, use those to teach the multiplication tables.

Divide Sheets

Working math problems can be overwhelming for some students to whom math does not come easily. Have students fold their sheets of paper in half when doing an assignment, so they only see the top half first. When they are finished, they work through the bottom half of the page. This makes the work more palatable for students.

Color Coding

Color code operational words like add, subtract, multiply, and divide. When students need to add, they use red pencils. For other operations, they use a different colored pencil. This helps them remember what they are supposed to do. When students start to work division problems with multiple operations, give them each a problem with colored blanks so they know which operation to do next.

Learner's Remorse

Always assess math learning in a way that separates it from the student's language ability. Students may know the answers for math but may not be able to read written directions or understand oral directions to do the problems. Make sure that students know what you need them to do. When you are in doubt about a student's comprehension of instructions, have that student work only one problem. If you see the student is on track, the student continues to do more. This practice prevents learner's remorse. This is a term I use for when students learn a task incorrectly and repeat it incorrectly several times. After students repeat a task incorrectly, unlearning the habit and relearning it correctly is difficult. They have learner's remorse, which can sour them for future learning.

A CONCLUDING STORY

Many years ago I had a college professor who told us a story about his graduating class. He said that he was part of a large graduating class, but the person who got the highest grades in his class was a student with LD. That student had more of one ingredient than all the other students did. He did not have the highest IQ, the most financial wealth, or the best looks. He had something better than all the others, and it was motivation. That motivation kept him searching to find ways to succeed, to graduate at the top of his class. You, too, can do this for your students. You can give them the motivation that they need to succeed. Believe in them. See something that they do not yet see. And after a while, they will see it, too!

How to Handle Anger and Oppositional Defiant Disorder

3

Anger is one letter away from danger.
—Maryln Appelbaum

When I am speaking to audiences, teachers across the country describe students as being more angry and violent than ever before. I can vividly remember the day I went do an inservice training for an elementary school on the West Coast. There had been a shooting that resulted in the death of a student the day before I arrived. The teachers and administrators were all visibly frightened. I was frightened too and wondered if it would happen again while I was there. At other times, I have gone to schools where I have had to go through airport-like security just to enter the building. The world has changed, and there are more angry students now (Overstreet, 2000).

Angry students can and often do create chaos. They create crises everywhere—in halls, gyms, cafeterias, and classrooms. Situations can easily escalate and become out of control. Students seem to have more access to weapons and sometimes bring knives or even guns into schools. Other students are frightened and try to avoid angry, hostile students. Students and faculty who do not even know the angry students may have heard about them and also adopt a fearful attitude, avoiding all angry students. They, too, become angry—angry at the students with anger issues and angry at themselves for not being able to stand up to them. Still other students enjoy watching students become angry, and they set them up so they can see the anger emerge.

Is anger really a bad thing? The truth is that everyone reading these words has at some time in their lives been angry. Anger is a normal emotion. However, when it is expressed inappropriately, it becomes a problem.

Anger is a secondary emotion. It occurs after feeling one of the primary emotions—fear, frustration, powerlessness, worthlessness, unfairness, hurt, or loss. The primary emotion occurs first. Here is a story that clearly illustrates this point. Melissa told her mom she was going over to a friend's home. Her mom, Mrs. Wilkins, was busy with a project for work and told her to be home at 5:00 p.m. The time flew by, and at 5:45, Mrs. Wilkins looked at the clock and realized Melissa wasn't home. Mrs. Wilkins started to get worried. She decided to wait until 6:00 and then start making some calls. At 6:00, Melissa still wasn't home. Mrs. Wilkins started calling the neighbors asking for Melissa. She couldn't find Melissa anywhere. By now, it was nearly 7:00. Mrs. Wilkins got in her car and started driving around looking for Melissa. She couldn't find her anywhere. She came home and started calling local hospitals and the police. At 7:45, Melissa walked into the house. When Mrs. Wilkins saw her, she started yelling, "Where have you been? You are in big trouble!" Mrs. Wilkins was feeling anger, but it was a secondary emotion. The primary emotion was total fear that something bad had happened to Melissa. It turned out that Melissa was on her way to her friend's home when an elderly neighbor asked for her help because of a medical emergency. The time had flown by, and Melissa hadn't realized how late it was.

When students are angry, it's important to always think about what the primary emotion may have been. Was the student feeling frustrated about not being able to do work? Was the student rejected by peers? In some cases, the primary emotion may not have happened at school but at home or on the way to school. The student may have displaced anger (Denson, Pedersen, & Miller, 2006). Displaced anger is anger that is felt toward another person or circumstance.

Benjie was a student with displaced anger. Benjie is now a young adult. He told me that as a child, he remembers feeling very frightened every time his mother got sick. She was frequently hospitalized with life-threatening illnesses. Benjie couldn't show that he was afraid at home because he didn't want to make his mother feel worse in any way. Each time his mother went into the hospital, he acted out. He was angry and got in trouble. His feelings of fear and powerlessness translated into anger at school. No one connected with him to find out what was happening at home. The situation continued until secondary school, when one of his counselors realized what was happening. They talked, and she taught him new and more appropriate ways to handle his primary feelings.

Displaced anger also occurs in children who are being abused at home. They are terrified of the abuser and cannot say or do anything at home. Some of the students internalize the anger and become depressed. Others come to school with displaced anger and let it out on others.

Your goal is not to stifle the anger that students have but, instead, to help them to express it in a healthy way—a way that helps them express the primary emotion too. There are positive benefits of anger expressed appropriately. It provides a sense of release for students. It also clears the air so that others understand what is going on.

Not all students have displaced anger. Some students express anger because they are copying family members. Children grow up watching how their role models express anger. They see them yell and shout and even hit something. If children see adults rage and berate others when angry, that is what they learn as the appropriate way to express anger. They don't know any other way, so they do what they have seen, even if they didn't like it and even if they themselves were the victims of angry people.

In addition to family role models expressing anger, children also see role models in the media expressing anger (Anderson & Bushman, 2001). Students watch more television today than ever before. They see acts of violence in television programs on a daily basis. They see actors and actresses showing sarcasm and little respect when speaking to each other. They see people being killed and maimed as a way of getting retaliation and revenge. The news is filled with stories of violence. Children rarely see programs that teach restraint and problem solving in a peaceful way. They also play video games filled with violence. While children are playing those games, they routinely "kill" or erase people. That is how they win the game—by making others disappear.

Today's students are more stressed than ever before, and this is a contributing factor to anger in students (Bagdi & Pfister, 2006). They are frequently rushed from one activity to another. They have very little opportunity to "blow off steam" with spontaneous play in their neighborhoods. Instead, they hurry from lesson to lesson to learn karate, piano, sports, dancing, and computers. When they are home, they are often glued to their television sets watching violence and negativity. In school, there is often additional pressure, as more and more school districts are requiring students be taught to the test. Curriculums are so geared to the final state assessments that, in many cases, recesses have been cut, and so have more relaxing classes like music and art. The result is that students come into schools stressed to the maximum, making it more difficult for both teachers and students. Stressed students can, and do, lose their tempers more frequently.

Suppressing anger can cause psychological difficulties. Students become like cans of soda pop that have been shaken over and over again. Eventually, that soda pop can explodes. The seal pops off, and there is soda pop everywhere. It's the same with children who have been bottling up anger. It bursts forth in many ways. The student may burst forth as a bully and hurt others. The student may become depressed from holding the anger inside. The student may start building a false world to escape from the real world. These effects of anger are all things that you need to prevent in students. The goal is to help students express themselves in positive and appropriate ways.

THE STAGES OF ANGER AND STRATEGIES FOR EACH STAGE

Stage 1: The Trigger Stage

Anger does not usually just flare up. There are four distinct stages that I have observed over the years while teaching. I call them the Trigger Stage, the Turning Point Stage, the Firing Stage, and the Fall-Out Stage. Each stage calls for different strategies.

The first stage is the Trigger Stage. This is the stage in which students begin to become upset. They feel some type of primary emotion triggered by something upsetting. Students become upset, anxious, moody, and confused and may not be able to think clearly. This is the easiest stage to help students.

Greet and Read

Stand at the door and greet students as they enter the classroom. I did this when I was teaching. I smiled and said welcoming words. As I spoke to them, I "read" their moods. I checked to see if they looked happy, sad, angry, or worried.

When you greet and read students, you know what approach to take with individual students. Mr. Jenkins had attended one of my seminars and had learned to greet and read. One day, Mr. Jenkins was standing at the door to greet and read students. He noticed that one student, Tory, looked upset. Tory was seven years old and a happy, good-natured student. On this particular day, Tory looked different. He wasn't smiling. Mr. Jenkins made a mental note to talk to Tory as soon as he had the class organized. A short time later, Mr. Jenkins asked Tory if he was all right. Tory said that his parents had told him the night before that they were moving to another city. He was scared. He would have to make new friends and start all over again. Tory talked while Mr. Jenkins listened until Tory felt better. He had been bottling his feelings up inside, and the more he talked, the better he felt. It all started with Mr. Jenkins greeting and reading Tory.

Mood Sticks

Some students are harder to read. Mood sticks are an excellent way to detect if something is wrong. This strategy takes a little preparation, but it is so worth the time. You will need four small empty baby food jars or similar-sized containers. You will also need craft sticks or tongue depressors and large stick-on labels. Make a label for each jar. Mark them "Happy," "Mad," "Sad," and "Worried." Draw a little face to match the word on each label. Now, you are ready to involve the students. Hand out the craft sticks so that each student gets their own. Have them individualize the sticks with their names and their own individual art design. Place all the labeled craft sticks into a larger jar so that names are sticking out where students can see them.

When students enter the classroom, have them find their individualized craft sticks and place them into one of the mood jars describing their mood that day. You will immediately know the moods of your students so you can help them.

This strategy also has a bonus purpose. It is an easy method for taking attendance. The craft sticks left over in the larger bin are there because students are absent.

Moods are Contagious

This Trigger Stage is very important. It's the earliest stage in which you can nip problems before they escalate into full-fledged anger. Your job during this phase is to help students stay coherent. Do this by being patient and calm. Use a calm, soothing voice when speaking to students. Your mood is contagious. If they hear in your voice that you are upset, there is a greater likelihood that they will become more upset. This is not the time to insist on rapid compliance of low-priority issues. Power struggles magnify and intensify anger.

Caution With Transitions

Some students have a tougher time with change, including the changes that can happen in classrooms. Throughout the day, there are many transitions. One of the ways to minimize the impact of transitions is to have a schedule, a routine that is consistent. Students always know when the next event will happen. Warn all students ahead of time when there will be change. "In five minutes, it will be time to put your work away and get ready to go to lunch." Just saying these simple words can prevent students from becoming stressed and anxious at a sudden change and minimize angry outbursts.

Music

Music is a calming influence on the classroom (Hallam, Price, & Katsarou, 2002) and can be used to prevent problems from occurring. Play calming music as students enter the classroom. Play special songs when there are transitions. If the entire class is starting to get "antsy," put some music on, and the mood in the classroom can change within seconds.

Anger Rules

Have posted rules about expressing anger. For example, one rule can be: "It's OK to be angry, but it's not okay to hurt another student, property, yourself, or the teacher." This can prevent problems before they happen. Discuss the rules with students. Have them give you examples of why it is important to have these rules. The more they are involved, the more likely they are to follow the rules.

Taking Pulse

When students start to get stressed, their pulse rates go up. Mine does too. This is a strategy that I have used effectively on myself and taught others to do with students. Teach students to take their pulses. (Some will not find it, but they have a good time trying.) When you see students are beginning to get upset, have them lower their pulses by five beats. Students sit quietly with their hands on their pulses and breathe deeply to calm themselves and lower their pulses. There may be times when you ask the entire class to calm down and lower their pulses by five beats.

Choosing Color

Another calming activity during the Trigger Stage is to have 10 sheets of paper that are all different colors. When students feel angry, they browse through the colored sheets to find a calming color. When students find the most calming sheet of paper, they pull it out of the stack, sit down, and look at the paper while breathing deeply.

Talking About Feelings

One of my favorite strategies during this stage is to do what Mr. Jenkins did with Tory. He had Tory talk about what was bothering him—moving away. Talking provides an emotional release. Set up a mini-conference area within your classroom. Two or three cozy chairs grouped around a table provide a safe area for students to go when they need to talk to you. Because it is not possible to stop everything you are doing every time a student becomes upset, it is an excellent idea to have a special time each day for students to come and have a "mini-conference." They sign up in advance by putting their names in the mini-conference box. Call their names to invite them to their mini-conference. Some students may choose not to come. They feel better because time has passed or because simply asking for the mini-conference was therapeutic. They no longer need to actually meet with you.

When having the mini-conference, use effective listening strategies. Be on the child's level. This helps the child feel safe. Sit comfortably facing the student. Make eye contact if you feel this is comfortable for the student. (There are some students who are uncomfortable with eye contact. It would defeat the purpose of the mini-conference.) Show that you are listening by nodding your head and focusing your attention on the student.

Your goal is to listen and learn and to allow students to come up with their own appropriate responses to situations that are upsetting. This empowers the students. Help students identify their choices and choose the most appropriate response.

Anger Options Chart

Have students create an anger options chart. This is a procedure that takes several days to fully implement. On the first day, ask students all the things that make them angry. Record them all on a flip chart. The following day, ask the students all the ways they handle their anger both appropriately and inappropriately. They are not to stop and think about it, but they should instead brainstorm all the ways they handle being mad. Write everything they say on another flip chart and display it for them. On the third day, have the students look at the list they made of all the ways they handle their anger. Remind them of the anger rules: "It's OK to be angry, but it's not OK to hurt another student, property, yourself, or the teacher." Ask them which strategies they listed comply with the anger rules. List these on a separate sheet called the anger options chart. They now have a list of ways to express anger appropriately in the classroom. The class can add to the list during the school year if they think of other appropriate strategies. Now when students are in Stage 1, the Trigger Stage, they can look at their options and know the most appropriate one for them.

Stage 2: The Turning Point Stage

I call this the Turning Point Stage because this is a turning point for angry students in determining how to express their anger. The primary emotion has been unresolved, and now they are almost ready to burst out in anger. This is a critical stage because it is your last chance to respond to the students' feelings in a way that facilitates communication and resolution. It is a stage in which it is still possible to reach students. There are strategies you can use to help students so that their anger does not escalate into rage.

Push Pause Button

Students are very familiar with remote controls for their television sets. They know that each remote has a Play button and a Pause button. When they push the Pause button on the remote, the program they are watching pauses. When they are ready to watch more, they push the Play button. Have a remote control in your classroom that is not connected to a television or other media. Remind students that it has a Pause button. Tell them that when they are feeling angry and want to explode, they can take the remote and push the Pause button. They continue to hold the Pause button while breathing deeply until they feel better. They then release the Pause button, push the Play button, and go back to their classwork.

Mood Duster

Have a feather duster in your classroom. They are inexpensive and can often be purchased at dollar stores. Keep it in a special place. Explain that when a person becomes angry, the person often feels the anger everywhere. A way to calm down before saying or doing the wrong thing is to take the feather duster and "dust off" the anger. Demonstrate dusting yourself off gently with the feather duster. Students enjoy this simple yet effective strategy because it provides a visual for them to remove the anger from their minds and bodies. It's really cute to watch a student to do it and then afterwards say, "I feel all better now."

Relaxation Station

Have a cozy place in your classroom designated as the relaxation station. Add warm touches like a rocking chair, soft pillows, and relaxing pictures on the wall. Some teachers use landscapes or seascapes for the walls. Other teachers use positive sayings like "I'm in control." Involve the students in choosing decorations for the relaxation station. Add some blank pages and colored pencils that students can use to write or draw their feelings. Headphones with relaxing music make a nice finishing touch.

Limit the amount of time students spend in the relaxation station, or students will spend too much time there relaxing instead of doing their work. Have a timer, and when the timer goes off, students return to their regular classroom routines. Some students will have to be redirected following the relaxation station to ensure that whatever they were doing was not the impetus that frustrated them in the first place.

Calming Bag

Create calming messages for students. Messages can say, "Count to ten backwards," or "Go to the relaxation station." When students are upset, they reach into the calming bag and choose a folded message on how to cool down. To make the calming bag even more special, have students write the calming messages.

Turtle Time

Discuss with the class what a turtle does when it is upset. The students always respond that the turtle goes within its shell. Ask them to show you what that looks like with their body language. They generally tuck their head down on their desks, fold their arms, and tuck their feet under their chairs.

Talk about what happens when the turtle feels safe. Students will say that it comes out of its shell. Have students demonstrate doing this too. Tell students that they can engage in this same strategy. When they feel angry and upset, they can say to themselves, "It is turtle time." They fold their arms, tuck their heads down, and take some deep breaths. When they are feeling calm again, they start moving around as they come out of their protective shells like a turtle. It is a very calming technique because it gives students permission to go within and calm down. This is a strategy that they will remember for their entire lives.

Stage 3: The "Firing" Stage

During this stage, students are so completely overwhelmed by anger and frustration that they lose the ability to think rationally. They have lost control. It's called the Firing Stage because they fire off, spouting off inappropriate words and behaviors. The target of this anger may be another student, school property, the teacher, or even themselves. They may lash out and hit someone or something. I have seen students bang their heads against a wall, pull their hair out, jump up on furniture, and try to hit teachers. I vividly remember one youth who was so angry, he was incoherent. He took his house keys out of his pocket and threw them across the room. The keys hit a planter on his own desk. It broke into many pieces, and that frustrated him more.

Caution Responding

This is not the time to try to reason with students. Don't touch them to calm them down because they may turn on you, and you may get hurt. Trying to approach students or talk to them during this phase only increases their frustration. They are in a critical phase and can't respond to what you are saying in a logical way. I have had students who reported afterward that they don't even remember what they said or did while they were in this stage.

Pre-Arranged Student

If you know in advance that you have students who continually fly into rages that can be harmful to others, set up a signal with one of the other students. When that student sees you give the signal, the student leaves the room and goes to get help. This needs to be a discreet signal so that it does not further upset the raging student. If there is an emergency button in your classroom, this is a good time to push it.

ABCD Technique

It's very important that you stay calm. The calmer you are, the calmer other students will be. Talk to the class calmly and reassure them. Have them keep doing their work. If they have no work at the moment, give them an assignment. They will take their attitude from you.

The ABCD technique is an excellent way to become calm. The letters are used as a reminder for each of the four steps in the strategy.

A stands for "arrest yourself." Stop. If you say something in the heat of anger, you may regret it later.

B stands for "breathe." Take some deep breaths. When people become upset, they tend to breathe shallowly into their chests. This increases rather than decreases stress. Take a deep breath into your abdomen. Hold it for a few seconds and then slowly let it out. Do this several times.

C stands for "calming statements." Say calming statements to yourself. The words that you say to yourself about situations can profoundly change your attitude and then your actions. Say phrases like, "I am calm;" "I can handle this;" "I breathe deeply and become calmer and calmer."

D stands for "do it again." Do it over and over until you know that you are calm. Then, and only then, are you ready to act.

Stage 4: The Fall-Out Stage

After students have lost their tempers, they are typically exhausted from their own rage and anger. Some students do not even remember what they said or did in the heat of anger. Others may be embarrassed and experience remorse. Still others are glad that they expressed themselves and may even feel that others "had it coming." Now is the time to step in and ensure that this does not happen again.

Making Restitution

After the student calms down, it's time to do some damage control. If the student broke something, it's important that the student finds a way to restore the property. This can take a long time. A good example of this is Adam, who was one of those students with a great, mischievous smile, huge dark eyes, dark wavy hair, and an outgoing personality. He was frequently in trouble with his teacher. I was the principal of the school at the time, and he was in and out of my office. One memorable morning, I walked into my office to find Adam. He stood there with a tiny bottle of white correction fluid in one hand and the brush from the bottle in the other hand. As I looked around my office, I quickly saw that my wooden desk was now decorated with white correction fluid. My black telephone had white dots. My computer had white streaks. My green Parsons table had white dots. I never knew there was so much correction fluid in such a tiny bottle!

Adam saw me and stood there, caught in the act. He started shaking and yelling, "I didn't do it! I didn't do it!" I was so upset that I could barely speak. I took some deep breaths and said in a low, deep voice, "You did do it, and now it needs to be fixed." He immediately threw himself on the floor and had one of the biggest tantrums I have seen in my years of teaching. He yelled, "I hate you! I hate school!"

It took a while for Adam to become calm. When he was finally calm, we had a mini-conference. I said, "Do you want to tell me about it?" I did not ask, "Why did you do it?" I had learned over the years to never ask a student, "Why?" Students typically don't even realize why they do what they do. Sometimes, they would rather make up a story than tell the truth. It's much better to ask, "Would you like to talk about it?" It's a good question that opens the door to more honest communication. Adam told me that his mom had given him some new medication that morning for allergies, and he felt out of control. He also said that he was angry at having to come to my office. As we sat and talked, I was impressed by how articulate he was. When we both felt better, I told him that I still had a problem with all that white in my office. I asked him if he had any suggestions to make my office look good again. He told me he would clean it all up; however, he was embarrassed that other students would see him cleaning. I suggested that he could come in earlier in the mornings, before school started. We checked with his mom, and she said it was fine. Adam and I really bonded over the course of the next week as he cleaned off all the white correction fluid.

Making Amends

If the angry student hurts another student, it is important that the student who was angry make amends. This does not mean being forced to apologize. When students are forced to apologize and do not feel remorse, they are lying. They are learning to lie to get out of trouble. Amends is different. It is finding a way to make it up to the injured student. The students together discuss ways the angry student can make amends. It may be helping the injured student do a project. There have been students who have become good friends as a result of this intervention.

No Arguing

When students become calm, take charge and do not argue. Arguing turns into power struggles in which there are winners and losers. You are the teacher, and therefore you are in charge of the classroom. You have a choice—a choice whether or not you want to get into a struggle with students.

When you get angry with students and allow them to push you over the edge, they learn that they can win. They can push your buttons. Once they learn they can push your buttons, they will continue to do so over and over again. It becomes a game for them called "get the teacher." The more frustrated you become, the more they enjoy the game.

Pre-Arranged Signals

Have a mutually agreed upon signal for students when they show signs of anger. The signal is a reminder to calm down. The signal can be something as simple as making the symbol of the Peace Sign by forming a V with the forefinger and middle finger. The signal can be given to only one student or to the entire class.

Calming Environment

Prevention of problems is a major goal. Look around at the classroom environment. Check out the colors in the room. Colors can carry a powerful message. There are some colors that are calming. Pink inhibits the release of hormones that contribute to aggressive behavior (Walker, 1991). It lowers blood pressure and rate of respiration. Have lots of pale pink in your room, especially in the relaxation station. Bring in a floor lamp from home or purchased at a garage sale. Add a pink bulb to the lamp to create a calming effect. You will find that it is especially effective in classes with students who are aggressive and unruly. Avoid having too much pink, as it is so calming that students will feel sleepy. At one seminar I gave in a hotel, my meeting room was changed to a restaurant. The restaurant was only open at night and had pink lighting to create a better atmosphere. It was very difficult for me to keep my audience members awake because I, too, was so relaxed that I felt like taking a nap. A little pink lighting will go a long way.

Sky blue is another color that is calming for students. Blue fosters respect, responsibility, and knowledge (Wagner, 1985). Sky blue releases neurotransmitters that are calming to students.

One-on-One Solutions

Help students find ways to "not fire." They need to think about other strategies they can use in the future for becoming calm. What works once may not work the next time. Have them make their own individualized anger options charts. If they feel their anger escalating, they get out their charts and determine what will work best to regain self-control.

Anger Log

An anger log (see Figure 3.1) is an effective way for students to analyze their anger so they can learn new methods of handling conflict situations. Students complete this form when they are calm. They write about the events that occurred that were the triggers, how they handled the anger they felt, and what they can do in the future to ensure this does not reoccur.

Figure 3.1 Daily Anger Log

Date _____ Time _____ Place _____

What happened? _____

_____

_____

My primary (underlying) feeling _____

_____

Did I hurt: *(Check one or more)*

☐ Someone

☐ Something

☐ Myself

How others probably saw my expression of feelings _____

_____

_____

How could I have expressed myself more appropriately? _____

_____

_____

What can I do to make the situation better now? _____

_____

_____

What will I do in the future when angry? _____

_____

_____

Self-Talk

Self-talk is what people say to themselves about any situation. People use it from the minute they get up in the morning until they go to bed at night. In the morning, self-talk might be something like, "It's raining outside. It's going to be a gloomy day." Self-talk occurs when you look in the mirror and say to yourself, "My hair looks great today. I really like the new gel I am using. I think I will buy more."

When angry, self-talk can be statements like, "I'm so mad. How could she do that to me? I feel like hitting something." Self-talk is effective for teaching students self-control (Kendall & Treadwell, 2007). Positive self-talk has words like, "I can handle this."

Teach students how to use self-talk. Start by demonstrating it. Talk about an upsetting situation and then make a self-talk statement: "This is upsetting, but I can stay in control." Do this about several different situations, changing the self-talk statement each time so that it is appropriate to the situation.

Have a list of positive self-talk statements. These are similar statements to the ones that are in the calming bag, except that they are printed on a sheet of laminated paper. Do a class exercise in which students discuss situations they find upsetting. They choose self-talk statements from the list that would help them stay in control. Have them get into dyads and practice telling each other the upsetting situations and then discussing with their partners the self-talk statements they will use. They then role-play the situations, and instead of getting upset, they use self-talk.

Figure 3.2 Self-Talk to Control Anger

"I am getting calmer every minute."

"Easy does it."

"This is upsetting, but I can stay in control."

"I'm on top of the situation, and it's under control."

"I can handle this calmly."

"This is a great opportunity for me to stay calm and in control."

"I am not going to get bent out of shape. I can handle this."

"Don't make more of this than I have to."

(Continued)

Figure 3.2 (Continued)

"As long as I keep my cool, I'm in control."

"I breathe deeply and stay in control."

"This doesn't have to be a catastrophe."

"I am calmer and calmer every minute."

"I stay in control of myself."

"I don't like this, but I don't have to stretch it into an awful situation."

"I am calm and in control."

"Breathe, breathe, breathe . . . stay in control."

"I think of something else that calms me down, and then I can easily handle this situation."

"I'm relaxed and confident."

"I never, ever lose my temper. I think carefully before I speak, and all is well."

OPPOSITIONAL DEFIANT DISORDER (ODD)

It is really important to be able to distinguish students who are angry from those who have oppositional defiant disorder (ODD). ODD is a chronic condition and creates major problems for those who have it and for the people in their lives. I am including it in this chapter because I feel it is important for you to know and understand this disorder in case you ever encounter it.

One of my dearest friends married a man with ODD. He had told her that he had a Jekyll-and-Hyde personality, but hearing about it was not the same as living with it. When he was kind, he was very kind. When he raged, he really raged. She never knew when it was coming. She eventually divorced him. It took her months to recover from a marriage of walking on eggshells. That is what often happens in classrooms. Teachers have students with severe anger issues and do not realize that it is ODD. The teachers walk on eggshells, never knowing what to expect from these students.

Figure 3.3 Symptoms of Oppositional Defiant Disorder

☐ Easily annoyed and irritated

☐ Easily frustrated

☐ Ignores directions

☐ Dislikes rules

☐ Refuses to comply with requests

☐ Disobeys authority

☐ Argumentative

☐ Persistently insists on having own way

☐ Defiant

☐ Deliberately annoys others

☐ Blames others for mistakes

☐ Sensitive

☐ Lack of ability to be flexible

☐ High maintenance

☐ Sees things in terms of black and white

☐ Outbursts

☐ Difficulty controlling temper

☐ May break or destroy things when angry

☐ May harm self when angry

☐ May use obscene language

☐ Moody

☐ Extremely compliant about some issues

☐ Has Jekyll-and-Hyde personality

☐ Negative

ODD is a chronic, persistent, negative way of handling frustration, anxiety, and anger (American Psychiatric Association, 2000). It is persistent in that it has to last for at least six months before it can be called ODD. This is because people go through periods in their lives that can be difficult and they may react in strong ways that resemble ODD for short periods of time, but it eventually goes away. ODD does not go away.

Students with ODD handle their anger far differently from the way other students who are the same age and even from similar cultures handle anger. It is interesting that within classrooms, ODD does not immediately show up. Students with ODD may start out behaving appropriately, but once they get to know their teachers, they typically and frequently defy them and annoy both teachers and other students.

Students with ODD are quick to anger. Anything can set them off, so they go right to the "firing" stage. They are provocative and initiate confrontations with rudeness, lack of cooperation, and general resistance to those in authority. This is not the same as conduct disorder, where students generally violate the law and the basic rights of others. Students with ODD do not violate the law or rights of others, but ODD can develop into conduct disorder if it is not treated. There are specific medications that can be used for ODD, as well as classroom strategies. Some of the strategies you have learned here will also help you with students with ODD.

Medical Management

This is a very real disorder, and there are medications that are beneficial. I have personally seen the difference they can make in students with ODD.

Moods are Contagious

It's important that you remain calm even when students are provocative. They know exactly how to push your buttons. Even if they succeed in provoking you inside, do not let them see it on the outside. I often say at seminars, "Fake it until you make it." Your mood is contagious, more contagious than a cold, so stay calm. Your mood will set the tone for the entire class.

Signals

Develop signals ahead. Students with ODD are generally very strong-willed, so for the signals to be most effective, they need to choose them. The more involved they are, the more invested they will be in having the signals work.

Anger Options Chart

Ask them for ways they can remain calm even when they feel provoked. The anger options chart is effective. When they make their own individual options charts, they are once again most invested in having it work.

Appropriate Expressions

Children do not know it, but they are often starved for ways to express themselves. When they don't know appropriate ways, they engage in inappropriate ways. I went into a classroom recently and instead of just observing to help the teacher, I met with the students. They were great! They told me their behavior issues. They were each aware of them. I then offered suggestions. It was a wonderful experience because the entire class was chipping in to help each other and bounce back with what would work or not work with different students. Several of the students had problems with aggressive behavior. They did not know how to deal with situations that aroused feelings of frustration, hurt, and disappointment. I gave them as a class lessons in social skills. You can do this too.

Asking for Wants and Needs

When students do not know how to ask for what they want, they may act out. They need appropriate wording. Teach them to say, "I would appreciate ..." when asking for something. Have them role-play asking for what they want. "I would appreciate getting to work on that project with you." This gives them a way of asking respectfully, rather than getting argumentative or combative.

Positive Expectations

The more you believe in students, the more they will believe in themselves. Teach them to think positively about what they can do. Some students feel like failures. They have been told over and over again that they are "ragers" and out of control. Talk about the fact that what occurred in the past can stay in the past. They can start over again. Give them hope that they can succeed. Most of all, remember this is a real psychological disorder. If you see signs, it is important to seek help for the student.

How to Handle Bullying 4

*Sticks and stones and words can break bones of the body
and the spirit.*

—Maryln Appelbaum

Bullying has become more and more of a problem in schools in recent years. Fifteen percent of students are either bullies or victims of bullies. It doesn't matter if schools are large or small, the ethnic composition of the school, or the school setting. Bullying can and does occur in all settings (Banks, 1997).

A bully is defined as a person who repeatedly harms others over time through direct attacks like teasing, taunting, threatening, and hitting or through indirect attacks like spreading rumors, intentional exclusion, and social isolation. Boys generally use more direct attacks, while girls use more indirect bullying methods. At seminars I hear increasingly that girls are now engaging in more direct physical attacks, too.

Bullying can occur by one person, or there may be a team of people all involved in bullying one or more victims. Students who are targeted all have in common that they are physically, verbally, or socially weaker than the bully (Hazler, as cited by Carney & Merrell, 2001).

Students who are bullies generally need to feel powerful and in control. They seem to obtain satisfaction from inflicting suffering on others and have very little empathy. When questioned about bullying, they think their behavior was reasonable and defend their actions, saying that their victims provoked them. Bullies typically display no anxiety about what they are doing. They may lie to defend themselves, steal, taunt, and show cruelty to animals. Some bullies become involved at young ages in substance abuse and sexual behavior ("Bullies and Their Victims," 2001).

Victims of bullying are not the social butterflies of the school; rather, they are the opposite. They are typically anxious and insecure, lack social skills, have few friends, and feel socially isolated. They rarely defend themselves, and they rarely retaliate. School is a place to be feared because it is unsafe. Bullying can lead victims to feel depressed, lower their self-esteem, and carry over into adulthood. There are some students who are so victimized that they plan and carry out acts of retribution against not only bullies, but also others in the school. This has been the case in many school shootings, including the shootings at Columbine High School, where the shooters had been victimized for years and had reached the point where they wanted to strike back. Columbine and other school shootings involving victims of bullying clearly demonstrate the immensity of the problem.

Bullying impacts the bully, the victim, and the entire school. A strong correlation exists between being a bully during school years and experiencing legal or criminal trouble as an adult. Sixty percent of students who bully in middle school have at least one criminal conviction by the time they are 24 years old (Olweus, as cited by Banks, 1997). Students who chronically bully others usually also bully when they are adults, having a negative impact on their lives. Developing warm and caring positive relationships is difficult because others withdraw from students who are chronic bullies.

STRATEGIES FOR UNDERSTANDING AND HANDLING BULLYING

Bullying interventions need to involve the entire school, not just the perpetrator and victim. Programs for both bullies and their victims must be in place, and those who are victims need to learn that they do not have to remain victims (Dess, 2001).

Bully-Free Classroom

Start your anti-bullying program by having a bully-free classroom. Conduct class discussions about bullying. Ask questions like, "What is bullying? What happens to people who are bullied? How do you think bullies feel? What's it like to see someone get bullied? Who would like to have a bully-free classroom?" Then discuss having a bully-free classroom. Establish some rules to set the tone for a classroom that is bully-free.

Students all offer suggestions for those rules (Beane, 1999). Examples of those rules can include

- We treat each other with respect.
- We speak up if we see others being treated unfairly.
- We like it that people are all different.
- We treat each other the way we want to be treated.
- We have the right to be safe.

Call your classroom bully-free. Involve students in making posters to hang up around the room, declaring it a bully-free classroom.

Figure 4.1   Bully-Free Classroom Sign

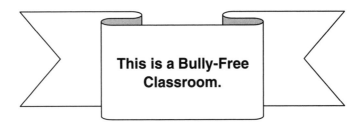

Bully-Free Pledge

Create a classroom pledge that students say each day. The pledge is a constant reminder that this is a classroom and a school that are bully-free. It reminds students who would be bullies not to bully. It also puts an end to the "spectator effect" that occurs when students watch other students being bullied but do nothing.

Figure 4.2   Bully-Free Pledge

We will not bully others.

We will help others who are bullied.

We will include students who feel left out.

We will report bullying.

We are a caring community.

Bully Box

Students who are victims are often terrified to tell their teachers that they are being bullied. They are scared that the bully will harm them even more, so they need a safe way to report bullying. The bully box is a safe way for students to report bullying without fear. Students who are bullied or who see bullying occur can write about the occurrence and place it in the bully box. They can even do it anonymously. The bully box needs to be in an area of the classroom or school that is easily accessible, yet is also private so that students can go there without being embarrassed or frightened. I saw one school's bully box in the school library. Even though you have a bully box, also have a designated person, someone safe, someone that students trust, to whom students can talk (Garrity & Jens, 1997).

Climate of Caring

Teach students about kindness. Discuss all the ways they can be kind to others. Have a special time each day to talk about the acts of kindness that occurred during the day. Start a kindness chain. Write the acts of kindness on six-by-two-inch strips of colored construction paper. Adhere them together in an interlocking chain and hang them all around the room. The goal is to have the kindness chain spread out from one end of the room to the other.

Role-Plays

Role-plays are a powerful method for teaching new behaviors. Victims and those who watch bullying without doing anything about it (bystanders) all learn new skills for handling bullying. Make up stories for the role-plays. Include bullies engaged in bullying, a victim, and bystanders watching the bullying. See the following sample role-play that you can use with your class.

Posture

Students who are victims are generally not the type of students who stand up for themselves with their words or in their stature. Teach them how to walk tall. Have them practice standing straight and walking. Provide activities that hook their interest to help them feel better about themselves. Assign them peer buddies so they don't feel lonely. The goal is to help them feel better about themselves and to have them walk tall.

Figure 4.3 Sample Role-Play

Eight-year-old Thomas was on the playground during recess. He was standing by himself, trying to look invisible. Other children were playing around him. Two eleven-year-old boys came up to him and started barking like dogs. Thomas did not know how to respond. He nervously giggled. One of the boys said, "Hey, stupid, that is what you are. You are a dog." Thomas could barely breathe. He could hear the pounding of his heart. The two boys kept on barking, and then they started making comments about how short Thomas was, calling him a "little squirt." They made fun of his height, short legs, and little fingers. Thomas was too scared to tell them to stop. He wished he was safe at home. Other kids were watching. One other boy came over and joined in the bullying. Finally, recess was over. Thomas was a nervous wreck all day. He was too scared to go to the restroom for fear one of those kids would come in. He was worried about walking home after school. He could not concentrate on his schoolwork.

Questions for Students

If you were on the playground and overheard this, what would be something courageous you could do?

Does Thomas have to go through this bullying because he is shorter?

How do you think Thomas feels?

Has this ever happened to you?

What are some things that Thomas can do?

What do you think of the boys who bullied Thomas?

How could you help the boys who were bullies to never bully again?

Developing Leaders

Vinny was tall and muscular and had long, dark, slicked-back hair and dark eyes. He was very bright and could do his work faster and often better than most of his peers. He had other students gathered around him before class, after class, and especially during recess. I noticed that students were around him but seemed scared of him. He had another side to him, one that was often sarcastic. I also started noticing that there were some kids who avoided him altogether on the playground. One day I discovered why. I found Vinny bullying Howie, a student who was very tiny for his age, who was shy, and stuttered when he spoke. I broke up the bullying and decided to investigate what had happened.

I discovered that Howie was not the only student Vinny had bullied. Many students were terrified of Vinny. I was the school administrator, and I knew I had to do something. After thinking about it for a few days, I had a private mini-conference with Vinny, who thought he was going to be in big trouble. He was surprised when I said, "You know, Vinny, I have been watching you. I see that other students listen to you." He nodded his head in agreement. I continued, "I think you have natural leadership ability. The kids all listen to you attentively when you speak in and outside the classroom." Vinny again nodded his head in agreement. He was more and more interested in what I had to say. I said, "I would like to work with you and develop your leadership ability. I think you can go on to become a real leader in the community. Who knows, you might become mayor, senator, even president some day." Vinny listened even more attentively. I told him, "I would like to give you a role in the classroom, a time each day during group time when you get to start practicing your leadership. How does that sound to you?" Vinny nodded his head. He was totally absorbed in this conversation. I continued, "Great. That is what we will do. Of course, as a leader, you will have to be a role model of appropriate behavior so that others learn to copy that behavior. That's what leaders do—inspire others to do the right thing. That's the kind of leader I want to help you be. Is that OK with you?" Vinny nodded his head and agreed. And that was the start of a whole new way of behaving for Vinny. We involved the class, telling them that he was a leader-in-training. At first, some students may have been frightened, but soon they really enjoyed this new side of Vinny. He had channeled his leadership abilities into something positive.

There's an even greater ending to this story. Vinny and I stayed in touch. He invited me to his high school graduation and, later on, his college graduation. I was invited to his home following the graduation ceremony. He showed me his scrapbooks and how he had been named most likely to succeed. He was president of his senior class. He proudly talked about his accomplishments to me, and then he said, "But you know, I will never be elected president of the United States." I said, "Why not, Vinny?" He said, "Because I am foreign-born." I told him, "Vinny, for you, they will change the laws." You just never know how the words you say can make a difference in the lives of children. He had remembered my words to him from so long ago. That is what you can do, too. You, too, inspire students to be better, to channel the leadership abilities that they are using to bully, to instead be positive leaders. Every day you get to make a difference in the lives of students. You are a difference maker.

How to Handle   5
Students With
Bipolar Disorder

Teachers are the anchors for students on the ship called Hope.
                                        —Maryln Appelbaum

A t a meeting of one of the local psychological associations, the speaker was a top-notch psychiatrist who has been conducting research on bipolar disorder and depression. I had already learned much about bipolar disorder, and I was interested in what he had to say. When I first started learning about bipolar disorder many years ago, it was said that people do not show any symptoms until the age of eighteen. (In those days, it was called manic depressive disorder.) In recent years, however, bipolar disorder has inched its way up to being a frequently diagnosed disorder in young children. I was very interested in what the psychiatrist thought about this. He spoke about symptoms and about the newest medications. He answered a few questions. He did not address bipolar disorder in young children. I approached him afterward and asked him what he thought about children being diagnosed with this disorder. He told me that just as with ADHD, he believed that while many diagnoses were valid, many were invalid.

It is true that there are some children with bipolar disorder, but as I describe to you the symptoms, I want you to know that it takes a professional to make the diagnosis, and even then, they can make an error. There is a lot of discussion in the world about racial profiling, an assumption that all people who share a similar race are the same. There is no talk in the world about psychological profiling, assuming that every child or adult that shares similar characteristics actually has a disorder. Be cautious in how you approach children who you suspect have this or any other disorder. There are some psychologists and psychiatrists who believe that it does not truly exist in children (Smith, 2001). There may be a variety of reasons why children act as they do. I know that I am not at my very best when I don't take care of myself, sleep enough, and eat well and when I am under stress. For some children, it could be as simple as that. For other children, it could be a real disorder. Twenty to sixty percent of adults with bipolar disorder report having had some symptoms as children (Smith).

The diagnosis is often complicated by the fact that many children with bipolar disorder have ADHD. Some symptoms of the two disorders overlap, including motor restlessness, distractibility, difficulty following through on tasks or directions, interrupting, and lack of attention to details (Jimenez, 2000). Some children with bipolar disorder are diagnosed as having ADHD and are treated with stimulant medication. If these students have bipolar disorder, the stimulant medication may make them more manic.

It is very important to have an accurate diagnosis (Duffy, 2007) because children with bipolar disorder can suffer serious consequences if they do not receive appropriate medical treatment. Children may engage in reckless behavior, which may lead to self-injury, hospitalization, and even attempted suicide. Moreover, without treatment, students will have difficulties in both their home and school relationships because of their reckless behaviors and mood swings.

Signs of bipolar disorder can begin as early as infancy. See Figure 5.1. Babies may be more difficult to care for and less predictable. As these children grow older, they may have severe separation anxiety and extreme moodiness and irritability. They engage in disruptive behavior that gets worse and worse along with temper tantrums and an inability to handle frustration. Outsiders look at their behaviors and find them strange and extremely emotional and cannot figure out why their moods change for no discernable reason. As students swing between high-energy mania moods and depression teachers may notice extreme moodiness and irritability that is very visible and disruptive for the classroom.

While many students are talkative, children with bipolar disorder in the manic phase talk a lot and talk differently (Biederman et al., 2000). They use pressured speech, speaking extremely rapidly, firing off one thought after another, and it's difficult to keep up with what they are saying. The speech may or may not make sense, as they often illogically jump from one idea to another as their thoughts race together.

I was recently asked to consult with David. He was a really nice-looking child with a great smile, a happy attitude, and lots of enthusiasm.

Figure 5.1 Checklist of Early Signs of Bipolar Disorder

☐ Unpredictable

☐ Severe separation anxiety

☐ Violently dislikes transitions and new situations

☐ Temper tantrums

☐ Increasing behavior problems

☐ Extreme moodiness

☐ Extreme irritability

☐ Sleep problems

☐ Aggression followed by remorse

☐ Declining academic performance

☐ Impulsive

☐ Lack of concentration

☐ Inability to handle frustration

☐ Hyperactivity

☐ Extremely emotional

☐ Mood swings

☐ Delusional thinking

I asked him what he was interested in, and that was all it took for him to launch into a long talk. He started telling me about building something in his room, then jumped to getting his parents to buy the wood and how it expensive it was, how he loves to eat steak, how cows are sometimes too skinny, and that he has been sick lately and that his doctor said he has something called bipolar disorder, but he doesn't want to take the pills, and he hopes his family doesn't catch his house on fire because once he set the house on fire. He said all of this within minutes. As I sat there listening to his pressured speech, I felt my heart go out to this bright student. I asked him why he wouldn't take his medicine, and he cited what I have heard so often. He didn't like how he felt when he took it. He said, "It doesn't feel like me. I hate it."

During periods of mania, students generally behave as David did. They are in constant motion and frequently restless. He could not sit still. His foot was constantly moving. When he talked about setting his house on fire, he was demonstrating yet another characteristic of bipolar disorder; students with this disorder may engage in daring feats of behavior that can cause harm to themselves and to others. They may believe they are unstoppable, like they can do anything. I had an acquaintance whose husband was diagnosed with bipolar disorder. He thought he could fly and jumped off the top level of an atrium hotel to his death. This is a serious disorder and must be treated so that lives can be saved.

Students with bipolar disorder have drastic mood changes, sometimes rapidly, between being manic and then sinking into deep depression. The depressive states are totally the opposite of feeling manic. They are debilitating. They are characterized by persistent sadness, worrying, anxiety, and lack of energy for normal activities. Students can barely get themselves to school and may have a "Who cares?" attitude. They can't concentrate or make decisions because everything seems so overwhelming. They withdraw from friendships and other relationships. The depression may be expressed as anger, irritability, and agitation. Students may have recurring thoughts of death and suicide. In fact, suicide is a real threat in individuals with bipolar disorder.

When adults have bipolar disorder, they may stay in a manic state or a depressive state for days or weeks before cycling. Children, on the other hand, can cycle rapidly between manic and depressive states, often in minutes or hours. This makes it hard not only on the teacher and classmates who never know what to expect, but also on the students who feel they have no control over their emotions. They are correct. They do not have control over their emotions. This makes living with bipolar disorder a very painful and lonely experience.

STRATEGIES FOR SUCCEEDING WITH STUDENTS WITH BIPOLAR DISORDER

Medical Management

The first step in managing this disorder is to get an accurate diagnosis and start the child on medication that can help the child have control over mood swings. The medication used for bipolar disorder is typically a mood stabilizer and sometimes an anti-depressant. This medication needs to be taken on a regular, consistent basis. Frequently students with bipolar disorder do not like taking their medication. Like what happened with David, students start taking the medicine and do not like its calming effects. They are used to those periods of mania in which they get lots of things done, and they don't want them to end. Additionally, students may feel so good when taking the medication that they believe they are cured and stop taking it. The symptoms then reoccur. Medical care needs to be consistent, and medication needs to be monitored.

Structure

Students with bipolar disorder need structure. They need consistency and routine to reduce the opportunity for mood swings. Watch out for unplanned changes in routine, as this can trigger a mood change.

Mood Diary

Because mood swings are a constant problem, it is useful for students to track their moods. Teach students to keep a mood diary so they can predict their moods. A pattern may emerge that will help students prevent mood swings. Have them record each day's major events and their moods afterward. I have seen students and teachers learn to predict the mood swings. Kim felt tired, and she said her thoughts felt like they were in slow motion right before she became depressed. Sidney became talkative, speaking rapidly, and that was a cue that he was about to go into a manic state. Some students cannot see their own cues, but when they have a mood diary, both you and the students can start to see patterns emerge.

Cozy Retreat

When students are particularly irritable and emotional, a cozy retreat can help calm them. One of my favorite ways to create a really quiet, cozy retreat was to take a table, put it in a quiet area of the room, pop a few cozy pillows under it, and partially cover it with a nice frilly tablecloth. Students liked it so much that I had to set up some rules about it. I placed a liquid timer next to the pillows and told students that they could flip the three-minute timer two times before they had to come back into the classroom. (If students were having a really bad day, they could come to me to negotiate a longer stay.) I also had the "one student, one bracelet" rule. I attached a little hook to the table and hung a woven bracelet on it. When students wanted to go into the retreat, they put on the bracelet. This was a signal to other students that someone was already on retreat. When a student finished being in the retreat, the bracelet had to go back on the hook so other children could take a turn.

Goal Setting

Goals help students stay focused. Have students set goals and write them down. The goals have to be something they really want. Just having that goal in sight can help them through the ups and downs of this disorder. It helps them feel they can succeed. It gives them a purpose.

Sleep

Getting proper sleep is important for everyone, but it is especially important in maintaining mood stability. Even individuals without bipolar disorder have a hard time functioning without sleep. Students with bipolar disorder may have extreme mood fluctuations if they go two or more nights without sleep.

Offering Hope

Have you ever gone through a tough time when you felt like you could not control your mood? I have. In one year, my mom, my best friend, and my little dog all passed away. I thought I handled it pretty well, but sometimes, I just would see something or hear something that reminded me of a loved one, and I would get really sad and sometimes start to cry. I did not plan to get sad. It just happened. What got me through this period was the caring of the other people in my life. Imagine being a student with bipolar disorder and not being in control of your moods. They, too, need lots of support and encouragement.

All students are sensitive to the words you use. Positive words are much more effective than negative. Use positive wording with students and avoid anything that can make students feel bad for their moodiness. Bipolar disorder is a real illness. It cannot be seen like a broken limb or glasses or a hearing aid. It can only be seen in the moods of students. It's important to stay positive so that they, too, can stay positive.

Pet Care

If it's at all possible, have pets in the classroom. When students take care of pets and hold and hug them, it is soothing. If your school does not allow live pets, substitute a class stuffed animal. Give the stuffed animal a name and make it come to life for the children. They can have special clothes for it for different seasons. They can take turns taking it home on weekends and journal their activities with their new friend. Even older students enjoy having that stuffed animal. They may laugh and be silly when introduced to their new friend, but it is amazing how much of a difference it can make.

Stop Sign

Make stop signs out of construction paper. Students can help color the hexagon and write the word "stop" in the center. Place the stop signs on the desks of students who need to calm down. Make sure it is in a place where they can easily see it. It serves as a visual cue to take some deep breaths and calm down.

Movement

Students need to move when they are feeling restless. Send them on errands, even within the classroom. "Jemitha, I need you to carry this book over to that shelf. Thank you so much."

Stressbusters

Involve the class in some stretches to get exercise and provide movement. Do some deep breathing together as a class. Play calming music or fun music—music that is mood changing. The less stress students experience, the better they can feel.

Outside Help

Finally, if all of these strategies on any given day are not enough and you see that students are getting either very manic or appear really depressed, send them to the nurse's office. A change may need to be made in medication. These students need extra help, and the nurse can help them get the help they need. Severe depression is very serious. It can lead to suicide.

Suicide is a real threat for students with bipolar disorder. If a student talks or hints about suicide, take it seriously. I vividly remember the first student who mentioned suicide. I immediately reported it to the psychologist, and it turned out that this student had already plotted out the details of how he was going to take his life. That one action saved his life. Be vigilant. You can help save a life. Look also for other symptoms, including withdrawing from friends, an inability to concentrate, dramatic changes in personal appearance, and loss of interest in favorite activities. Watch also for expressions of hopelessness and guilt, preoccupation with death, and giving away favorite possessions. If you see any of these symptoms, get immediate help for these students. You may be helping to save lives.

How to Handle Students With Autism Spectrum Disorder

6

I can remember rarely hearing about students with autism spectrum disorder (ASD). That has dramatically changed in recent years. In 2000, when the American Psychiatric Association wrote about autism, they cited the incidence as five cases in ten thousand. Now, it is estimated to affect one child in every one hundred fifty (Jepson, 2007). That is a dramatic increase, which is why it is important for everyone who works with students with ASD to be armed with both an understanding of this disorder as well as classroom strategies to help students.

ASD falls under the umbrella of a disorder known as pervasive developmental disorder (PDD). There are distinct characteristics of all individuals with PDD. They all have severe problems with social interactions and communication skills and typically also have maladaptive atypical behaviors not commonly seen in others (American Psychiatric Association, 2000).

Students with ASD have a triad of deficits in social reciprocity, communication, and repetitive behaviors or interests. All of these can range from mild to severe. They affect the ability of students to communicate, have social interactions, and perform in an educational setting (Stuart, Flis, & Rinaldi, 2006). You can usually see this in the classroom in delays or abnormal functioning in language and in social interactions.

One of the most amazing facts about ASD is that in 20 percent of families, children started out with language skills and seemingly normal social interactions (Jepson, 2007). Then, sometime in the first or second year, children either stop talking or start engaging in unusual behaviors. I have spoken to many stunned parents. They tell me that they had no idea there was any problem, that their children were fine, and then, *wham*, their children seemed to totally change. It is heartbreaking to hear the stories from these families. Still, other families saw problems right from the start and say that there was never a normal period of development.

The symptoms of this disorder are different in all children, who fall on a spectrum of mild to severe. The spectrum may include mental retardation that also ranges from mild to severe. Children with ASD are almost always more interested in objects than in people. This is characterized by a persistent preoccupation with objects that can include buttons, paper clips, rubber bands, and pencils. If the object moves, they may be even more fascinated by it. They may become preoccupied with fans or spinning wheels on toy cars. Kyle was one of those children. He was totally absorbed by the wheels on toy cars. He sat for hours, spinning them back and forth. He also liked boxes and jars. He would open them and then close them, open them and close them, over and over again. Some children's fascination with objects extends to their own bodies. They become preoccupied with their belly buttons, arms, or legs. They may swing their arms back and forth or in a circle repeatedly.

Another typical behavior is an insistence on sameness. Even the smallest change in the environment can provoke a tantrum. It can be as small as changing the time by five minutes for lunch, lining up at a different place to go to recess, or changing the silverware used at lunchtime.

Children with ASD also have a need for repetition. Just like a spinning object, that same need for repetition is shown in other behaviors. They may again and again line up a group of objects for no apparent reason. They may repeatedly imitate the actions of someone in their lives or even of an actor they saw on television. Their hands may flap repeatedly, their fingers may flick, or they may clap their hands repeatedly. They rock back and forth or sway. This can look even more unusual because of odd body postures like walking on tiptoe or stooping while walking.

All of these behaviors can profoundly impact their relationships with peers. They generally lack eye contact, are not spontaneous, and have an inability to share in fun or even the achievements of others. They often need help in developing peer relationships.

Their speech may be delayed or nonexistent. Even if they do speak, the rate, tone, and pitch of their speech may not sound normal. Their grammar may be immature, and their speech may be filled with repetitive words— words that do not fit the conversation. Moreover, their words generally do not match their gestures and body movement. They may not understand directions you give or questions you ask. This deficit in language and communication skills can be a huge hindrance to their development.

This is a devastating disorder for so many families. I recently spoke to one mother of a boy with autism. She told me how her son had started developing normally. He made eye contact, was affectionate, and was starting to speak. When he was nearly one year old, he started to be more fascinated with objects and stopped making eye contact. He did not want to be held or touched anymore. His language not only stopped progressing, but it went backwards. This mom found herself in the autism loop, trying to get help for her son and desperate for some answers. This desperation occurs in many families. The students need your support and so, too, do the families. The students leave you at the end of the day and at the end of the school year, but the families have them forever and need all the help they can get for these very special children. The good news is that effective strategies do exist. You can also teach those strategies to families so that they can use them at home. The more you are a team, the better for your classroom and the better for parents and their children.

STRATEGIES FOR SUCCEEDING WITH STUDENTS WITH ASD

Structure

Once again, it is vital to have structure. Students with ASD thrive on sameness, routine, and consistency. Any change in the schedule or routine can result in maladaptive behavior, ranging from a mild tantrum to head banging.

Consistent Routines

Use systematic and consistent ways of carrying out tasks. It helps to have a routine of "first work, then play." They get used to having the fun activities after the work activities. Routines help to minimize memory and attention problems. Students always know what to expect and when to expect it. Routines also have the bonus of helping students compensate for their language delays. They do not have to ask or be told what to do. They know. They have learned the routine, and they know what to do and when to do it.

Left to Right, Top to Bottom

This drive for sameness extends to everything, including the layout of shelves in the classroom. Have items in learning centers in sequential order of use from left to right and from top to bottom. This prepares them for reading because books are written in this format, top to bottom and left to right.

Clear Visual Areas

Students with ASD are easily distracted, and it's important to have an area free of all distractions for students to learn. Choose an area of the classroom for seating that is simplified to minimize distractions. Have individualized study carrels. Ensure that the students do not feel isolated from others as they work. They need to feel they are an integral part of the whole class team, yet have the privacy they need to focus.

Individual Work Systems

Help students become and stay organized. Have all materials in the same place at all times. Have a system so that they know what work needs to be done first, what needs to be done next, and what needs to be done after that. Number or color code the system. For example, when students finish their work in box one, they move to box two and continue in this fashion. If numbers are a problem, get students accustomed to colors. Color boxes are an organized and efficient method to help students complete their work. They have three boxes, and the first is red. Students open the red box and complete their work there. When they are finished, they put the work on a tray. They then open the yellow box and complete this work. When they are finished, they put this work on the tray. Finally, they open the green box, remove the work, and complete it. When finished, they put their work on the tray and open each box to make sure they are all empty. They take the tray over to a special place on the teacher's desk, and they are ready to move to a fun activity like a puzzle. This becomes a ritual—a routine that they follow every day. The boxes are organized from left to right in the order that they are to be completed.

Do not assume anything about their work. Students with ASD need to be shown in a sequential fashion where to start on a sheet of paper. They need to be shown how to know when work is finished. There may be a mark at the bottom of the paper. When they reach that mark, they know they are through.

Visual Systems

Students with ASD process auditory information with difficulty and have more strength in the area of visual-spatial processing (Lincoln,

Courchesne, Harms, & Allen, 1995). This means that they do well with pictures. Use visual prompts for everything from teaching routines to having smoother transitions (Dettmer, Simpson, Myles, & Ganz, 2000).

Wrist Bands

Make student wrist bands and attach small cards with symbols and words to them using Velcro. When students need something, they turn up the appropriate card on their wrist band and show it to the teacher. If they want to get something from their backpack, they turn up the card that says the word "backpack" with a picture of a backpack next to it. They go to their teacher and point to the card. If the student wants to go to the bathroom, there is a picture and a word on the card so the teacher can understand what the student wants. This fosters independence and helps students to be able to communicate in a visual manner.

Everyday Needs and Objects

Another way to use pictures is to make pictures of everything you think students may want. Teach students to hand the picture to you—to actually place the picture in your hand. When the student does this, say, "You want the ..." and hand the student the object requested.

Visual Prompts

Use visual prompts for helping students line up. Make circles or squares out of construction paper and place them on the floor so that they lead toward the door. Teach the students to line up on the construction paper prompts. As students learn where to stand to line up, gradually remove the prompts so that eventually they do not need them at all (Heflin & Alberto, 2001).

Sign Language

Use visual strategies for communication. Teach them sign language. It gives them a way to both speak and listen. If you do not know sign language, use gestures. Use specific gestures to signal different activities. For example, make the peace sign with your fingers to signal it is time for everyone to stop working and be still.

Concrete Objects

Concrete objects can be used to help students communicate and express themselves. Teach them to hold and squeeze a stress ball when they are angry and upset instead of hitting themselves or others. Have them use a puppet to demonstrate what they want. They take the puppet to the water source when they are thirsty. They take the puppet to the pencil sharpener when they need their pencil sharpened. They can even take their puppet over to another student, and it is a signal that they want to be with that student.

Staying on Task

Keeping students with autism on task can be a challenge. Lengthen the time they are on tasks by ensuring they know something good is coming upon completion of the task (Egel, 1981). This can be something tangible like a sticker, or it can be a highly preferred activity. In order to get to do the highly preferred activity, students have to first do the less preferred activities (Azrin, Vinas, & Ehle, 2007).

Alternate Movement and Sedentary Activities

Plan the day so that a variety of activities are scheduled (Munk & Repp, 1994). Alternate between activities with high levels of movement and activities that are more sedentary (Prizant & Rubin, 1999). Some students need to engage in sensory-arousing activities like jumping and spinning prior to learning. Once finished, they are ready to calm down and learn.

Classroom Arrangement

Arrange the classroom so there are clear boundaries and designations to differentiate areas (Anderson, Campbell, & Cannon, 1994). Establish boundaries by putting visual markers to indicate different areas of the room. Keep in mind proximity issues. Some students do not like to be in close proximity to others. These students need additional space so that they can focus on instructional tasks.

Indirect Lighting

Use of indirect lighting may be more calming to someone with an easily overstimulated visual system. Bring in a lamp from home to warm up an area in the room. Be careful to not seat students directly under fluorescent lights.

Individual Learning Styles

When planning the curriculum, always base it on the student's individual characteristics, not on the fact that the student has ASD. Make sure materials are motivating. Observe students to see how they learn best. While it is true that students with ASD share some similar characteristics, they still are each unique.

Concrete Teaching

Teach skills in a highly structured, one-to-one format, providing clear and concise instruction. Speak simply and directly. Be concrete rather than abstract. Use short sentences. Begin with verbal prompts and physical guidance and then gradually use less and less guidance as students learn to complete tasks themselves.

Looking for Causes of Inappropriate Behavior

Before getting upset when students misbehave, it's important to understand the reasons behind misbehavior. The misbehaviors may be ways that students "talk" to tell you something is wrong. For example, tantrums can really be a sign that students are angry, or they can also be a signal that students are frightened. Look at what was happening right before the tantrum, and it will become clear. Walk up to the student and acknowledge what is happening. "It looks like you are really scared." Your words become the words that students wish they could say, and this often defuses the tantrum.

I can still remember the first student with autism that I ever had. There were no labels for any of the students in those days. I just knew that something was different. Every time he got upset, he would knock his head against a wall—the same wall every time. I was really frightened that he would hurt himself. Finally, I understood what was happening. He would engage in head-banging every time he got frustrated with educational instructions or when he wanted something from one of the other students. I started using my own words for him, "It looks like you don't understand the assignment." He stopped and looked at me. I said, "I'll be glad to show you another way to do it. Let's go to your desk together." He took my hand, we went to the desk, and I showed you another way to do the assignment.

You have to "read" students and situations. Just like you read a whole book to understand the plot and the characters, you need to read students.

Look at the student. Is the student trying to tell you something? Is there too much going on in the classroom that is distracting and confusing? Was the student simply trying to get your attention? Once you have read the situation, you will know better how to handle it.

Minimize Waiting

Students who do not have ASD often have a difficult time waiting. Students with autism find it even harder. There are so many sensory stimulations that occur during wait times like standing in line. There are other students all around, some physically touching each other, as well as more noise than usual as students wait. This can all put students on overload. If you cannot totally minimize waiting times, then teach students something they can do that will keep their attention focused while they do wait. You may designate a specific spot for students to stand or something for them to hold in their hands while waiting.

Teaming With Families

Teamwork and consistency are important. The more home training students receive, the better students will function both at home and at school. Let families know that you care and that you want to make a difference with their children. They will be happy to know there is someone else who cares. It is not an easy task to be a parent of a student with ASD. Family lives are completely altered anytime there is a child with special needs. Knowing that there is a caring teacher for their children helps foster a sense of hope.

How to Handle   **7**
Students With
Asperger
Syndrome

Each child is worth the time it takes to transform a life.
—Maryln Appelbaum

Asperger syndrome (AS), like autism spectrum disorder, is also grouped under pervasive developmental disorders (American Psychiatric Association, 2000). It, too, affects social and communication skills, but it is milder. Students with AS generally have very good language skills in contrast to children with autism spectrum disorder, who may have little to no speech.

Hans Asperger first described this disorder in 1944, and it was only in 1991 that it was published in English. It is characterized by subtle impairments in three areas of development: social communication, social interaction, and social imagination. All of these are social skills that affect how students with AS are viewed by others. Because their behavior is different, they often seem to be odd and peculiar to other students. It's not uncommon for these students to be the victims of scapegoating, teasing, and bullying.

Just as students with autism spectrum disorder often have obsessions with objects, students with AS may also have an obsessive interest in objects or in subjects ranging from a fascination with cars or electrical systems to enthrallment with world religions or even a television program. They talk incessantly about their obsession.

The behavior of students with AS is often rigid and inflexible (American Psychiatric Association, 2000). They keep doing what they do, regardless of the result. Leonel was in Mrs. Kater's third-grade classroom. Mrs. Kater received a complaint from another parent of a student in the classroom. The parent said that Leonel continuously phoned her son, Matthew, and that she had had enough. She related what had occurred the prior evening. She was just sitting down to dinner when the phone rang. It was Leonel, asking for Matthew. She told him that Matthew was at karate lessons. He said, "OK." She hung up the phone, and before she could even make it back to the dinner table, the phone rang again. It was Leonel, again asking for Matthew. She told him again that Matthew was at karate practice, and again, he said, "OK." She hung up the phone, and he called again and again and again. This is a classic example of rigid and inflexible behavior. Students with AS, like Leonel, are often impulsive and have difficulty holding back a response. They cannot see the whole picture and, instead, become narrowly focused on one detail, which, in this case, was speaking to Matthew.

Students with AS are different from students with autism in terms of intelligence. Typically, students with AS have normal or even high IQs. They generally begin talking when very young, and often they have such a rich vocabulary that their parents think they are gifted (American Psychiatric Association, 2000). Many are so bright that they go on to high levels of achievement as adults, excelling in areas like math and physics.

In social interactions, students with AS may have inappropriate eye contact. They may look away when speaking so that the listener feels a lack of connection. This is complicated by the fact that students with AS typically have a difficult time understanding what others are feeling. They generally can't read emotions through body language, facial expression, and voice inflection, so they do not usually understand when someone becomes frustrated, sad, or upset. Even when told what the other person is feeling, students with AS do not understand how to handle what they are hearing. They may talk at length on a subject, rambling on and on, even if their listeners are bored. They don't know the listeners are bored because they can't read this in the other person. Their interests are limited, so they don't have a wide range of subjects about which to communicate. Moreover, if the topic has anything to do with other people and how they are feeling, students with AS are usually totally lost because this involves skills they just do not have—handling emotions. They cannot handle emotions in themselves, and it is even more difficult to handle emotions in others.

At the same time, students with AS are emotionally vulnerable. They want and need friends but do not know how to begin or maintain a

Figure 7.1 Characteristics of Asperger Syndrome

- Deficits in social interaction
- Lack of emotional reciprocity
- Intellectual abilities in normal or superior range
- Occurs more in males
- Inappropriate eye contact
- Needs sameness
- Limited interests
- May have poor motor skills
- Poor concentration
- Emotionally sensitive and vulnerable
- Often talks at length on some subject of interest
- Does not grasp that others may not be interested in same conversation
- Limited problem solving social skills
- Anxiety
- May interrupt or talk over speech of others
- Difficulty understanding feelings in self
- Difficulty understanding feelings in others

---

relationship. They are especially sensitive to criticism, perhaps because they have often heard criticism about themselves. Anxiety is still another factor that complicates their relationships. They may feel so much anxiety about social interactions that it can cause them to freeze even more when speaking and relating to others. (See Figure 7.1)

Bryan, a student in Mr. Finch's third-grade homeroom, had AS. He seemed to often be isolated. Other children did not choose him for activities. He just appeared different. When he was called on in class, he would start off answering Mr. Finch's question but then get distracted and start talking about cars. He was fascinated with cars, and he had a subscription to many different car magazines. He could tell others all about the different features on cars, their reliability ratings, and his recommendations of the best cars. One morning Mr. Finch decided to get the attention of all the students in a new way. He blew a whistle. When Bryan heard the whistle, he ran to the wall and hid his head in his arms against the wall. His anxiety level had been high even before he heard the whistle. The whistle put him over the top in anxiety so that all he wanted to do was run and hide. When other students started laughing at him, he felt even more miserable. He felt like he did not fit in. Fortunately Mr. Finch understood immediately what had happened. He gave the rest of the class an assignment to keep them busy. He went over to the wall where Bryan was trying to hide. Mr. Finch spoke very calmly and soothingly to Bryan, assuring him it was safe in the classroom. He took out the whistle and showed it to Bryan. He promised to not blow the whistle in the classroom anymore.

In this case, the anxiety was produced by an object, but it can also be increased by criticism and harsh words. Some students do not run over to a wall and hide; rather, they hide inside themselves feeling scared and anxious. These students need help and understanding so they can relax and feel good about themselves and the classroom.

STRATEGIES FOR SUCCEEDING WITH STUDENTS WITH AS

Calm, Predictable Routine

Change is frightening for all students, and students with AS may find it even more daunting. They need to be slowly prepared for all changes. Tell them ahead of time if there will be shifts in the routine so they can be emotionally prepared. Warn ahead of transitions, even if they are part of a predictable routine. Use phrases like, "In five minutes, it will be time to put your work away and get ready for lunch."

If you know ahead that you will be absent and there will be a substitute teacher, inform your students. Tell them the routine they will be following the day the substitute is there.

Be consistent in not only your routine, but in what you say. When you say something, follow through. Consistency is essential for students with AS.

Maintaining Calm

All students take their cues from you, but students with AS do it even more. They may not understand what you are feeling when you are upset, but they know something is different. Fear of the unknown can create even more anxiety.

Engaging Teaching

Make assignments fun. The more fun students are having, the less they will feel anxiety. Start with an introduction that makes students want to learn. Just as a good meal begins with an appetizer, give them an educational appetizer. Tell them what they will be learning in a way that whets their appetites and makes them want to learn more.

Chunking Lessons and Assignments

Break assignments into smaller chunks so that lessons are not overwhelming for students. The higher their anxiety, the less they can accomplish. When one chunk is completed, students take a breather and then go on to the next chunk. The breather can be a fun activity. A short break in which they do something else that is still part of the learning assignment can provide relief from working intensely. This means that students need more time for completion of lessons, but it is so worth the time.

Clear, Brief Instructions

Make sure that students understand what they are to do before they do it. Have them check for understanding by repeating the instructions back to a learning buddy or to you.

Caution in Speech

Be very cautious how you talk to students if they are doing a lesson incorrectly. Remember, they are especially sensitive to criticism. Even when you are tactful, they may interpret it as criticism, so choose your words carefully. Keep your focus on telling them what you want them to do rather than telling them what they did wrong. This keeps it a more positive social interaction.

Observation

Step in if students seem to be having any difficulty so they don't become overwhelmed. Walk around as students do their assignments and stop to help students who need help. This is an effective strategy for all of your students and is especially useful for students with AS.

More Time on Tests

Just as you may need to give students more time for completing assignments, you may also have to allow more time for tests. Remember, anxiety is strong, and it's even stronger during testing. Rename tests. Call them "opportunities." They are opportunities for students to see how much they have learned. Call quizzes silver opportunities. Use words like "golden" and "platinum" to describe other opportunities. The goal is to minimize anxiety. This will help all of your students. Many students know the information but then freeze when it is time to take a test. Simply hearing the word "test" is enough to put students into a state of frozen fear.

Student Interests

Take advantage of students' obsessive interests whenever you can by incorporating them into the lessons. For example, if a student is fixated on cars and you are studying history in the year 2000, have the student include in the unit information about popular cars in 2000.

Proactively Protecting Students

Students with AS are often the victims of teasing and bullying. They need to be protected, and the best way to do this is to teach students to honor the diversity of others.

Commonalities Rather Than Differences

Do exercises with the class so that all students are more accepting of each other. A powerful exercise is the "things in common" exercise. Students typically look for differences in all students and single out students who are different from others for teasing. Break the class into groups of approximately five or six. Appoint a leader in each group who will report back to the rest of the class the results from that group's exercise. Have students face each other and instruct them that they have three minutes to find ten things they have in common as the leader takes notes. Give them a one-minute warning so they know when it is nearly time to be finished. Have the leaders read their lists to the class. When they are finished, have students within the group all turn first to their right and then to their left and tell people on each side one thing they like about them. This is a great bonding activity that keeps students focused on what they have in common rather than what is different. It changes the whole tone of the classroom, as students start looking for things they have in common rather than differences.

Classroom Signs

Students are affected by their environment. Have signs in the room that foster caring. The more they see the signs, the more the signs become part of the classroom culture.

Figure 7.2   Caring Classroom Sign

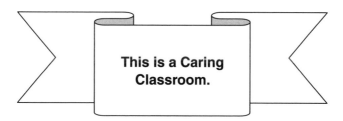

Teaching Social Skills

Students with AS typically do not have appropriate social skills. They need to be taught these skills (Cumine, Dunlop, & Stevenson, 2005). This includes how to ask for what they want and how to say thank you when they receive it. These skills do not come naturally. Rehearse with students over and over again until they understand and can do it easily. You can also use stories to teach social skills. Have them role-play different parts of stories and practice using skills.

Matchmaker Seating

Seat students near you so that you can ensure they are all right during the day. Act like a matchmaker, assigning students to be buddies with students with AS. Make sure the students you appoint are supportive and caring and enjoy helping others. The goal is for them to become classroom pals.

Stopping Obsessive Talk

When students with AS continuously talk about a topic on which they are fixated, other students can become annoyed. This creates social problems for the student with AS. Restrict the talk about the obsessive topic to a specific time of day. If the student starts talking about the obsession at another time, remind the student that there is a special time for talking about this topic. If the student talks on and on about the topic, change the subject in a gentle but firm manner. "Chase, you can talk about this later. Right now, let's all talk about ..." You can also use visual cues like holding up a stop sign. Students learn that when they see the visual cue, it's time to stop talking.

Stress Reduction

Teach students appropriate steps like deep breathing and counting to five to use when feeling stressed. Write the steps on a card that students carry at all times as a reminder. When they feel stressed, they get out their cards and read them.

> "I take five deep breaths."
> "I hold each breath to the count of five."
> "I feel better and better."

Visual pictures work well for stress reduction too. Have a set of relaxing pictures. They can include a sunset, the beach, the mountains, or other relaxing scenes. Involve students in helping you choose the relaxation scenes. When students are stressed, they choose a relaxation picture and look at it while deep breathing until they feel better.

Provide regular breaks during the day to engage in fun activities (Cumine et al., 2005). A short, regularly scheduled break can alleviate stress and help students focus better. During these breaks, it is good to provide movement activities like stretching.

Dare to Dream

Above all, when you are working with students with AS, have hope and patience. Be patient as you talk and listen to these students. Help them to feel they are a part of your classroom. Never underestimate the influence you have in their lives. Believing in them and taking time to connect and show you care can impact not only their present lives, but also their future lives. Teach them to dare to dream, to use the gifts they have to achieve all they can. Talk to them about people like Albert Einstein, who some believe had AS, who did succeed, who did make a difference (Rowe, 2003). Offer them hope and caring. You are a difference maker.

How to Handle Students With Tourette's Syndrome and Obsessive-Compulsive Disorder

8

A happy face comes from a happy heart. A happy heart comes knowing you are building better tomorrows for children.
—Maryln Appelbaum

CHARACTERISTICS OF TOURETTE'S SYNDROME (TS)

Tourette's syndrome is a neurological disorder characterized by tics (American Psychiatric Association, 2000). These are involuntary, rapid, sudden movements that occur repeatedly in the same way. There are two types of tics: motor tics and vocal tics. Motor tics are movements of the body that range from eye blinking to head jerking to abnormal body jerking. The second type of tics is vocal tics, which can range from throat clearing and belching to odd noises and speaking obscenities. The tics may occur many times a day nearly every day or intermittently.

Tics generally start when children are approximately seven years old. They typically begin with something much less severe like blinking, sniffing, or even cracking knuckles. Students may go through periods in which symptoms are continuously present and other times when all symptoms disappear for weeks or even months. They may feel relieved and think that they are permanently gone. It can be traumatic when they repeatedly return. It's like being on a roller coaster. They feel on top of their own world when the tics are gone, and then they come crashing back down when the tics return.

Students with TS do have times when they have some control over their symptoms. This can last for a few seconds to hours at a time; however, when they suppress them, they may be merely postponing even more severe tics. Students will say, "I have to do it!" They eventually have to express them and may become very embarrassed. They do not like to feel as though they are different from other students.

Tics occur more frequently when students are stressed. They generally decrease when students are more relaxed or when they are concentrating on something that totally absorbs their interest. For different types of Tics, see Figure 8.1.

Figure 8.1 Different Types of Tics

Motor Tics		
Eye blinking	Kicking	Throwing things
Eye rolling	Stomping	Tearing books
Squinting	Ankle flexing	Tearing paper
Head jerking	Table banging	Tearing cloth
Facial grimacing or contortions	Picking at lint	Squatting
Nose twitching	Lip pouting	Skipping
Body jerking	Lip licking	Stepping backwards
Hitting self or others	Lip smacking	Walking on toes
Clapping	Tongue thrusting	Twirling in circles
Kissing hand or others	Mouth opening	Knee bending
Pinching	Hair tossing or twisting	Foot tapping or shaking
Leg jerking	Arm flapping, flailing, or jerking	Foot dragging
Shoulder shrugging	Arm squeezing	Chewing or pulling on clothes
Knee knocking	Smelling fingers and objects	Somersaults
Stooping	Shivering	Body slamming
Jumping or hopping	Abdominal jerking	Scratching

Simple Vocal Tics		
Throat clearing	Yelling	Moaning
Grunting	Puffing	Saying unintelligible noises
Sniffling	Sucking	Saying words like "wow" or "hey"
Belching	Whistling	Guttural sounds
Spitting	Honking or hissing	Noisy breathing
Snorting	Laughing	Gurgling
Squeaking	Screaming	Calling out
Hiccupping	Shouting	Squealing
Coughing	Yelping	Clicking or clacking
Humming	Barking	Making "tsk" and "pft" noises

Complex Vocal Tics		
Repeating of phrases	Stuttering	Repeating ones' own words
Repeating words	Amplitude of speech	Repeating others' words, echolalia
Repeating parts of words	Talking to oneself	Speaking obscenities or socially taboo phrase
Animal sounds		

CHARACTERISTICS OF OBSESSIVE-COMPULSIVE DISORDER (OCD)

Obsessive-Compulsive Disorder (OCD) is a neurological disorder characterized by involuntary, recurrent obsessions and compulsions (American Psychiatric Association, 2000). These create anxiety, take up lots of time, and interfere with normal functioning. Obsessions are persistent thoughts, images, ideas, or feelings that students have. (See Figure 8.2) Everyone now and then may have persistent thoughts, images, and ideas, but these are excessive and generally do not make sense. The thoughts are so severe that students become frozen and can't do anything. They are literally stuck within their thoughts.

Compulsions are repetitive, ritualistic behaviors that are usually associated with the obsession. (See Figure 8.3) Students engage in the compulsions to relieve the tension, stress, and anxiety that are associated with the obsessive thinking. A huge majority of students with TS also have OCD.

OCD behaviors may increase or decrease, depending on stress due to events in the lives of students. These events may be emotional, physical, or environmental and are anxiety-inducing. Students become stuck and find it hard to function at different times.

Figure 8.2 Obsessions

- Focusing on cleanliness

- Focusing on exactness

- Needing to remember something

- Focusing on minor details over and over again

- Over focusing on one idea or action

- Focusing on the rightness or wrongness of a situation

- Focusing on specific numbers

- Focusing on certain colors for certain situations

- Being preoccupied with sensations that can include burning or cutting self

- Focusing on knives and scissors

- Extreme anxiety about harming self

- Extreme worry about harming others

- Worrying that something terrible is going to happen

- Over focusing on germs and illness

- Focusing on foods and eating

- Focusing on forbidden acts and behaviors

- Worry about aggressive impulses and images

- Focusing on behaviors that are forbidden

Figure 8.3 Compulsions

- Checking and rechecking amount of money
- Checking and rechecking if house is locked and windows shut
- Checking and adjusting clothes
- Aligning objects so they are a certain way
- Counting objects in a room
- Counting squares of sidewalk
- Walking without stepping on cracks in sidewalk
- Counting to a certain number prior to action
- Repeating actions over and over again
- Brushing hair a certain number of strokes
- Finishing a task once it is begun, even if time involved is excessive
- Inability to switch activities
- Repeating the actions others already did
- Repeating sounds and words to self
- Repeating numbers to self
- Asking the same question over and over again
- Concern with doing things perfectly
- Fear of harm coming to a loved one
- Picking sores, skin, nose
- Touching self sexually
- Touching others sexually
- Sucking thumb or fingers
- Biting nails
- Cutting self
- Burning self
- Repeatedly cracking knuckles
- Smelling self or objects
- Excessive hand washing, bathing, cleaning
- Writing and rewriting until paper looks perfect

PSYCHOLOGICAL CONSEQUENCES OF TS AND OCD

Serious issues can arise in students who have TS, OCD, or both. Students may have problems arriving at school on time because they are so busy at home with rituals (Purcell, 1999). They may be obsessed with perfection in all that they have to turn in. This obsession can cause them to do and redo their work. They may become embarrassed about being late to school and late turning in work. It is not a good feeling to feel different from others, so students with OCD often try to hide their rituals and thoughts from others. They may become depressed and discouraged and feel like they are crazy. This leads to even more discouragement and hopelessness. It also increases anxiety, which can increase their symptoms even more.

Their relationships with others may be impaired because of their symptoms and also because of their own oversensitivity and social embarrassment. It can cause them to go through periods of withdrawal from others. Self-esteem and self-confidence are lowered, and feeling unloved and frustrated is increased. It becomes a cycle of despair because the worse they feel, the more anxious they become, and the more anxious they become, the more their symptoms increase, creating further embarrassment.

STRATEGIES FOR SUCCEEDING WITH STUDENTS WITH TS AND OCD

Transition Warnings

Students with OCD cannot easily change tasks. They may have to complete the previous task before they can go on to the next one. Give them lots of advanced notice of transitions and shifts in activities. "In ten minutes, we will be going outside for recess. All work needs to be finished by then."

Structured Routine

Structure, routine, and consistency are recurrent themes throughout this book. Students need to know what will happen and when it will happen. A regular routine helps students realize that A follows B. They know what to expect, and it helps them stay on task.

Computers

If it is at all possible, have students with OCD work on computers. When they are working on sheets of paper with pens and pencils, they may make errors. When they make errors, they will sometimes erase the paper to the point that the paper is torn. They may start over and over again on other sheets of paper. It's so much easier on the computer if there is a mistake to erase and to make adjustments without having to start over again.

Group Projects

Help students not stay isolated (Purcell, 1999). Because they feel embarrassed and often secretive about their compulsions and tics, students tend to isolate. Assign group projects so that students get to meet and mingle with others.

Teaching Coping Strategies

You will have to adjust your expectations of students with OCD. This is a very real disability. Students may have to engage in a compulsive act over and over again before they finish their assignment. As long as you know this ahead of time, you can be prepared. For example, some students with OCD have a phobia of germs. They need to wash their hands over and over again. Their hands may become raw from so much handwashing; however, they still need to wash their hands.

Chelsie had OCD and TS. Mrs. Carlyle had her for second grade and observed that Chelsie washed her hands continually. She observed that every time Chelsie used learning objects, she always washed her hands afterward. One day, she noticed that while Chelsie was in the math area, she stopped what she was doing five times to go to the sink and wash her hands. Mrs. Carlyle also noticed that Chelsie washed her hands a lot if another student was coughing or sneezing. She washed her hands after she touched any foreign object like the door. Mrs. Carlyle spoke to the school nurse and asked her if she had any ideas. The school nurse recommended a brand of disinfectant that Chelsie could carry in her pocket and use whenever she wanted to wash her hands. Mrs. Carlyle met with Chelsie and told her that she had observed that a lot of time was spent in handwashing. She asked her if she would like another easier, quicker way to have clean hands that would not take time from class. Chelsie readily agreed, so Mrs. Carlyle explained how the disinfectant worked and asked her if she wanted one. Chelsie said, "Yes," and from that moment on in the classroom, she used her hand disinfectant. Chelsie still had OCD and TS, but she had learned a new way to manage her behavior.

Class Assignment Assists

Students with OCD may need extra time on task (Purcell, 1999). This is especially true if they do not have a computer. It takes them longer to complete assignments because of the fact that they are often compelled to check and recheck answers on both assignments and homework. Make sure that students have an erasable pen and extra erasers. You may also consider reducing the amount of classwork and homework. Students can become so frustrated when they feel overwhelmed that they stop and do nothing. In this case, less is definitely more. Less work to do can help students get more accomplished.

Seating

Do not seat students with TS in front of the classroom if students have severe tics. That can cause profound embarrassment for students. Seat students where they can still see and hear you yet will not feel like others are staring at them.

De-Stressing

Stress is a major component in symptoms. It is important to recognize that students with both TS and OCD need to have ways to de-stress. The less stress and anxiety they feel, the more they can get done.

Have a safe place for students to relax when they feel stressed. Use the relaxation station described in Chapter 3 for those times when students are feeling extreme stress. When they go there for a few minutes, it eases the stress so they can return to their seats and be comfortable and ready for work again.

Movement helps decrease stress. Ensure that students have both recess and physical education. Never ground students from having their special times for exercise.

Signals

When students are stuck in a ritual and cannot get unstuck, have a signal they can give for you to help them (Purcell, 1999). For example, they may have a special card in their desks with a blue circle. Whenever they are stuck and want help, they take the card out of their desks and put it on top so you can see it. It's a signal for you to help them and also a way for them to alleviate stress.

Organizational Skills

Teach students how to organize and maintain a neat and readily accessible notebook. Show them a visual sample of a notebook that is well organized. Attach to the inside of their desks a photo showing a well-organized desk and notebook. Provide times throughout the day for students to organize their materials.

Strategy Book

A strategy book is a collection of cognitive strategies and learning tricks that students accumulate over time. Every time students learn a new strategy, they place the strategy in the book. For example, when students learn a successful strategy for organizing a notebook, the strategy is placed in the book. When students learn how to organize a term paper, they place that strategy in the book. The book includes social skills, anger intervention skills, and relaxation skills.

Pro-Social Activities

Students with TS often feel isolated because of the stigma of having tics. Help to reduce these feelings by having peer partner activities and setting up a pro-social classroom in which diversity is honored (Carter & O'Donnell, 2000).

Understanding the Disorder

Be empathetic to the needs of students with TS and OCD. The more you understand how they feel, the better you will be able to accommodate them. For example, you may get angry when you think a student with TS is not listening. That student may be thinking, "My neck is jerking, and my eyes are blinking. The teacher has called on me and gets mad because she thinks I'm not listening." In reality, the student is so busy focusing on the tics that it is hard for the student to hear what you are saying. Still another student with OCD may be thinking, "I can't think about what Mrs. Jennings is saying. I am seeing an image over and over in my head of me getting ill if I don't get up and wash my hands. I have to sit here instead and listen, but I can't think about anything else. I sure can't focus on what is happening in class."

When students are feeling like this, it is nearly impossible for them to do what you ask. You can get their attention, but first you will have to help them relax. They cannot simply stop their minds. These are both real dis-orders. Medication will help, but it cannot take the place of an under-standing teacher. Talk to students in mini-conferences and ask them to think of ways they can focus more clearly. Many students have learned their own little tricks to help. Some students carry stress balls. Some wash their hands over and over again with disinfectant without standing up. Some have learned deep breathing. Some have a mantra they say over and over again to themselves until they feel calm and in control. For some stu-dents, help comes in the form of medical treatment and medication. But for all students, a caring teacher to help them on days when they feel out of control can change a rainy day inside that student's mind to sunshine. You are a difference maker.

How to Handle Students Who Are Disruptive

9

Students need encouragement like roses need sunshine.
                                              —Maryln Appelbaum

---

There are many ways students can disrupt the classroom. They may tattle, complain, blurt out, chatter, get into fights, and insist on having what they want, when they want it. Each type of disruption needs separate strategies and skills. This chapter will give you the skills you need to handle these hard-to-handle students and hard-to-handle situations.

SKILL ONE: HOW TO HANDLE TATTLING

Tattling is a very disruptive behavior (Gartrell, 2007). Students take up valuable class time when they tattle. They disrupt the routine and the consistency of the classroom. It is detrimental to promoting harmony and cooperation between students.

The origins of tattling are generally in the home. Children learn that when they tattle on a sibling, a friend, or another family member, that person gets in trouble. Children who tattle get sympathy and attention for the tattle. They also learn that when they have problems, adults will step in and solve their problems. They come to school and tattle for the same reasons. You cannot help what happens in the home, but you can help what happens in the classroom. Tattling can be stopped.

The first step in stopping tattling is to teach students the difference between tattling and reporting. Tattling is to get someone in trouble.

Reporting is when a student gets help for someone. Role-play tattling and reporting and have students tell you which one is being used.

- Jason tells you that Todd is hitting Scott in the playground and that Scott is bleeding. Is this an example of reporting or tattling?

  This is an example of reporting. Jason appears to be trying to get help for Scott.

- Tonya tells you that Sasha does not want play with her. Is this a report or a tattle?

  This is an example of tattling. Tonya appears to be trying to get Sasha into trouble. No one is getting hurt.

Have students give you other examples of reporting and tattling. The more they practice, the better they will get at recognizing the difference between the two.

Strategies for Success for Tattling

Staying Calm

Remain calm when you hear tattles. When students see that you get upset, it actually reinforces the tattling behavior. They think this is a way that they can always get attention and sympathy.

Tootles Curriculum

Set up a tootles curriculum. Tootles are kind statements that students say about others (Skinner, Cashwell, & Skinner, 2000). They are the opposite of tattles. Give students examples of tootles. "Kathy helped Ken when he dropped his backpack and everything fell out." "Al helped Elma understand their classroom assignment."

Have a special tootles time each day. Students report all the good things others did. When you hear a tootle, add a paper clip to a tootle glass jar. It needs to be clear glass jar so that students can see the effects of their tootles as the jar is filled. When the jar is filled with paper clips, the class has a tootles party. The class decides how they want to celebrate. Bring in a special treat and encourage them on that day to tell each other lots of tootles so that everyone leaves happy.

This is an effective strategy because it teaches students to say nice statements about each other rather than negative ones. The more they get focused on saying positives, the more the negatives fall by the wayside. It creates a completely different climate in the classroom.

Thanks

A simple and effective strategy for handling tattling is to hear the tattle and then say, "Thanks." Display very little emotion. Students learn from this that tattling gets no real sympathy or attention. They learn to handle their own problems and not get attention from trying to get another student into trouble.

Sounds Like

This is my favorite strategy for handling tattling. It acknowledges the emotions students have when they tattle and still does not reinforce the behavior. When you use this technique, you respond to the feeling the student has. You are using empathetic listening without getting actively involved. When Kenny comes to you and says, "Josh said a bad word," respond by saying, "Sounds like you're upset." Kenny feels acknowledged and heard, yet you did not get involved in resolving the issue.

Tattle Sandwich

A sandwich is composed of two slices of bread with something in the middle. A tattle sandwich is composed of two compliments and the tattle in the middle. If students want to tattle, they have to first say something nice about the other student. Then they say the tattle. After saying the tattle, they say something else nice about the other student. This forces them to think in a whole new manner about the students that they are trying to get into trouble. They are now looking for good things to say about these students.

Tattle Box

A tattle box is a special box set up in its own special place in the class-room. It is a place for students to write their tattles. They drop them into the box for the teacher to check. If the teacher feels there is a real cause for concern, then the issue is addressed.

Tattle Time

If tattling is a real issue in your classroom, set up a special time each day in which students get to tell their tattles. They cannot tell them before that time. By the time tattle time rolls around, they typically have forgotten all about the issue that had them upset in the first place. If they do remember the issue, they have to state it in the form of a tattle sandwich, saying two positives as well as the tattle.

Tattle Ear

There are some students who just like to talk about others. They are not reporting. They are tattling, telling one negative after another. Their goal is to get others in trouble. When students start to tell you tattles like these and are rambling on, have them go tell it to the "ear." Draw an ear and hang the drawing on the wall. Explain that this is the tattle ear, and they tell their tattles to the ear.

Tattle Report

This is an effective strategy for older students who tattle. Have them complete a report form. It is a detailed description of the tattle. By the time they are through filling it out, many students decide that it just is not worth the trouble to try to get someone else in trouble.

Figure 9.1 Tattle Report

Tattle Report

Tattler _____ Tattlee _____

Today's date _____

Tattle _____

_____

_____

_____

To Tattle or Not to Tattle

Students sometimes do not mean to tattle about someone else. They do it because they are having a problem with another student and just don't know any other way to handle the problem. Take time to teach students how to handle situations that are troublesome.

Teach them other methods to handle the situation. This is not the same as telling them how to handle the situation. When you tell them exactly how to handle situations, they are not learning to think for themselves and to take responsibility for their choices. Teaching them involves explaining different alternatives for the troublesome situation. For example, Lori comes up to her teacher and says, "Cindi is taking too long." Ms. Jenkins says, "You could say, 'Cindi, I would like a turn now,' or you could do something else until Cindi is finished. Which do you prefer?"

SKILL TWO: HOW TO HANDLE COMPLAINING

Complaining is similar to but different from tattling. It is similar in that students have formed a pattern of negative statements to get attention. However, it is different because the complaints may not be about other people but about situations. It is also different because students who frequently complain may develop victim mentalities. This occurs when students feel powerless about many issues. These students begin to believe that everything bad happens to them. They complain about everything (Parish & Mahoney, 2006). They say, "I can't," and actually stop trying to do things. They say they can't do their classwork. They can't do their homework. They can't do a partner activity. They can't be ready in time for a different task. They give constant negative excuses. They complain that assignments are too hard, that their parents are not available to help them, and that their classmates do not like them. It's important to break this negative pattern of behavior. Students all need to develop confidence in themselves. They need to learn their strengths and maximize them.

Strategies for Success for Complaining

"I Can't" to "I Can"

This is a really powerful strategy to teach students to say "I can," rather than "I can't." Begin by having all students in the entire classroom make a list of all the things they cannot do. Have an "I can't" ceremony. Students all take their lists and tear them up. The goal is to get rid of all the "I can'ts."

Next, get a dictionary. Find the word "impossible." Read students the definition. Tell them that in their classroom, starting now, everything is possible. Scratch out the word "impossible." Above it write the word "possible."

Tell students stories of people who refused to believe in the word "impossible." Beethoven was deaf, yet he composed beautiful music.

Einstein could not talk until he was four years old and had a very difficult time learning in school, but he went on to become famous for his theories. Tell students that these brilliant individuals have in common the fact that they never gave up. They never listened to the word "impossible." They believed, instead, that everything was possible.

Now, students are ready for the last step, and that is to have them make lists of all the things they would like to do that they previously thought were impossible. They prioritize the lists in order of what they will accomplish first. Every week, they scratch off items as they accomplish them.

Connect

One of the most important strategies for all students—those who complain, those who are shy and withdrawn, or those who are disruptive—is to connect (Parish & Mahoney, 2006). Every student needs to feel a sense of belonging. Students do not care how much you know until they know how much you care. When you take time to connect, it totally changes the dynamics of working with even the toughest student. Instead of constant bickering, nagging, and becoming frustrated, you will instead develop a completely new relationship with students.

One-to-One Meetings. Set aside a special time to meet with your toughest student daily for three consecutive weeks. The meeting needs to be for three uninterrupted minutes. Schedule the meeting for a time in which you can put your entire focus on the student.

This is not a time for you to do the talking. It is about getting to know the student. Start by explaining that you want this special time together to get to know the student better. Bring up a topic that you think will interest the student. If you are unsure, start with a topic that all students are interested in—a favorite television show, a favorite movie star, or a hobby.

Power Listening. When the student begins to talk, use power listening. Power listening is listening in a way so that students want to talk. It is very effective; I have used it over and over again with students. Sit so that you are both facing each other. It is best to be on the same level. As the student talks, nod your head to indicate that you are listening. Every now and then, say, "Really?" or "Hmmm." If the student describes something with lots of emotional impact, say, "Sounds like ..." plus the emotion. "Sounds like that made you angry." Your goal is for the student to keep talking. At the end of the time, thank the student and say that you look forward to doing this again.

At first, students will not understand what you are doing. They will wonder what your motives are; however, after a while, they will grow to like their special time with you. You will build a bond that is enduring.

SKILL THREE: HOW TO HANDLE CONSTANT CHATTER

There is a difference between the quiet buzz that takes place in the classroom when students are working together on a project and chatter (Bausman, Bent, & Collister, 1999). Chatter occurs when students are not paying attention and talking to friends or neighbors rather than engaging in their assignments. Chatter in the classroom is disruptive for the entire class. When one student starts talking, it becomes contagious for other students to be talking, and, soon, the entire classroom is talking. It's important to be stop chatter before it reaches this point.

Strategies for Success for Constant Chatter

Taking Charge

Start by taking charge of the classroom. Someone needs to be in charge. If you do not take charge, students will. Walk confidently. Speak with poise and confidence and believe in yourself and your ability to control the classroom. Students can feel when you are frightened and unsure of yourself. You may have to practice speaking in front of a mirror until your voice is strong, firm, and filled with positive expectations.

Fun Atmosphere

The more fun you have, the more fun students will have. They will want to pay attention to you because they are excited to see what you will do next. Your enthusiasm is more contagious than a cold. It is infectious. The truth is that any mood you have is contagious, so it is really important that your mood is filled with joy for teaching.

Silence Game

This is a method first devised by Maria Montessori when she was working with students in the slums of San Lorenzo, Italy. She used it to teach them the power of silence (Bettmann, 2000). It worked then, and it works now. Here's how it works. Tell the students that you will be asking them to close their eyes and listen. It will be for less than a minute. When they open their eyes, you will ask them to name all the sounds they heard.

They generally will hear the air conditioning or heating vent, others students' breathing, and noise out in the hall. The next day, do it again for a few seconds longer. Every day, do it longer and longer. It is amazing the sounds they start to hear that they never heard before. This game sets the tone for teaching students the value of silence. Some of them never experience silence. They go home, and their television sets are always on. The TV is even on when they go to sleep. They have grown accustomed to noise rather than silence. That is one of the reasons they chatter. With this game, you are teaching them to be still and enjoy the silence. It is a skill that will last their entire lifetimes.

Talking Without Sound

Have a special time each day when students can talk to each other without words. They make gestures but no words. Students look forward to this special time that is generally held at the end of the day as a fun time.

Chatter Box

Use a music box to keep track of time lost to chatter. When chatter begins, the music starts. When chatter stops, the lid on the music box goes down. At the end of class, play the unused portion of music. This is the time available for free talk. Students learn to save their talk so that they can have a longer, more meaningful free talk time. If you cannot find a music box, you can use a song on a CD.

Anchor Activities

When students have nothing to do, they may get bored. To entertain themselves, they may engage in inappropriate behavior. Have fun anchor activities for when students finish up their work and are waiting. Anchor activities are activities that fill up time in an appropriate way (Hipsky, 2007). Examples of anchor activities are puzzles, fun worksheets, fun reading books, and quiet games. Anchor activities provide a way to keep students busy having fun.

SKILL FOUR: HOW TO HANDLE BLURTING OUT

Blurting out occurs when students loudly say whatever it is they are thinking (Charney, 1998). It also occurs when they raise their hands to get the attention of teachers. They wave their hands frantically in the air as they yell, "Teacher, teacher!"

Strategies for Success for Blurting Out

Two-Hand Rule

The two-hand rule is a great way to solve problems with blurting out. Teach students that whenever they raise their hand, their other hand goes over their mouth. The hand over the mouth is a reminder to keep it closed until called upon. Have students practice using the two-hand rule. Ask them a question and have them raise their hands to answer you. During class time, if students forget to use the two-hand rule, gently but firmly remind them.

Avoid Reinforcing Behaviors

It's important to monitor your own behavior during blurt-outs. Do you call on students who blurt out? If you do, you are reinforcing the behavior that you wish to end. Every time you call on them when they blurt out, you are saying, "It's OK to blurt out. That's a good way to get attention." Be careful to avoid putting your attention on behaviors you do not want to reoccur. Whatever you put your attention on will expand and grow. Place it on negative behaviors, and they will expand and grow. Place it on positive behaviors, and they will expand and grow.

Hand Signals

There are times that students really do need to get your attention, and they need to do it quickly. If they need something that is urgent, have them raise their entire hand in a fist. The fist means that it is an emergency, and they need to speak to you immediately. You will need to define for them "urgent." If not, they may raise their hands in a fist all the time. Give an example such as students need to go to the nurse's office because they feel sick.

SKILL FIVE: HOW TO HANDLE TALKING BACK

When students talk back, it is not only disruptive, but it is also disrespectful. It sets a tone for other students to become disrespectful. It is something that has to be stopped before it increases.

Strategies for Success for Talking Back

Appointment Cards

It is important that you show students that you are the one who determines how and when disruptions will be handled, rather than the students. Set appointments with students to discuss the situation. Give the appointment card to the student and then resume teaching. During the appointment, teach students other ways to ask for what they want in a courteous manner. Have them role-play asking for what they want. Here are some examples of appointment cards.

Figure 9.2 Appointment Card 1

YOUR APPOINTMENT CARD

What you are doing is not appropriate. I need you to stop now.

Bring this note to me at _____.

Figure 9.3 Appointment Card 2

YOUR APPOINTMENT CARD

What you are doing is disruptive. I need you to stop now.
Write your plan for change in the space below.

Bring this note to me at _____.

My Plan

The problem is:

The reason for the problem is:

My plan is to:

Student signature: _____ Date _____

Teacher signature: _____ Date _____

SKILL SIX: HOW TO HANDLE POWER STRUGGLES

Power struggles are exhausting. A power struggle occurs when students want their way, and they hold out until they get what they want. It's a learned behavior. Students learn that if they hold out long enough, they can always get what they want. They generally do this not only in interactions with teachers, but also with their families. Family members typically describe these children as being strong-willed. They are strong in determination. This is an asset. It's important to not squelch their strength, but to teach them to be respectful of others.

Power struggles occur when students want what they want, when they want it, and the teacher wants them to do something else (Ferko, 2005). I can still remember at the beginning of my teaching career when this happened to me. I engaged in all the typical behaviors that did not work. I ignored the student and hoped the problem would go away. Sometimes, I yelled. Other times, I argued with students, and they argued back. Eventually one of us had to give in, and I'm embarrassed to say that often that person was me. I would just become so worn out that I gave in. As soon as I did this, of course, the student learned, "If I hold out long enough, I can always get what I want." The power struggles continued and continued with each one taking longer and longer to resolve.

Figure 9.4 Power Struggles Cycle

Student's behavior	Engages in inappropriate behavior Makes inappropriate request
Teacher's reaction	Ignores Argues Yells
Student's behavior	Additional inappropriate request or behavior
Teacher's reaction	Ignores Argues Yells
Student's behavior	Additional inappropriate request or behavior
Teacher's reaction	Gives in
Student's reaction	"I won" "This works"

Strategies for Success for Power Struggles

Appelbaum Rule of Three

It took a while, but I finally understood that I could not give in. I also realized what I now call the "Appelbaum Rule of Three." Every time you give in, you ensure that the student will engage in another power struggle at least three more times. That is because the student has won and has learned to hold out longer than you. The student will be convinced that this time will be no exception and will continue to struggle with you.

There are really no winners when this happens. Students may think they have won, but they have really lost. They have lost because they think they have learned something about the real world. In the real world, they cannot always have what they want, when they want it. That is not how it works.

One day, many years ago, I was on an airplane flying to give a seminar. I got into a conversation with a flight attendant. She was a very attractive, perky, 23-year-old woman. She asked me what I was doing because I had my notes out in front of me to prepare for the seminar. I told her that I was going to give a seminar on behavior management of children. She said, "Please tell my story." She then proceeded to tell me about her life. She said that as a child, she got everything she wanted when she wanted it. She said she would cry and have tantrums if she didn't get what she wanted. Her parents always gave in. She said that she started to have problems in her relationships in elementary school. She expected other students to also give her what she wanted. When they did not, she became angry, and friendships ended. She said that she had recently been engaged to a man she loved very much. She said she followed the same pattern with him, and he broke the engagement. To top it all off, she said that her parents had this past year cancelled her credit cards. They wanted her to make it on her own. She said she had no idea how to do that. She had taken this job, but she did not know if she would be able to keep it because her behaviors were so deeply entrenched. She ended her story by pleading with me, "Tell them my story. Tell them so that they know not to do this with children."

I do not know what happened to this young woman. One can only hope that she somehow made her life more successful. Her story is an inspiration to not give in to children all the time, to help them learn to be respectful, and to teach them skills that will last their entire lives.

Two Positive Choices

Typically, when there is a power struggle, teachers do offer choices. However, the choice is between a positive choice and a negative choice. It becomes a threat. "Do this or _____ will happen." This serves to make students rebel even more and hold out longer. When you offer two positive choices, students generally forget about their struggle and choose one of the two. "You can work on your math assignment now or read the current event. Which do you prefer?"

Students still feel powerful. They are still in control of what they do; however, it is between the limits you have provided.

Delaying

When students are extremely emotional about something, it is often wise to use the delaying tactic. This gives both of you time to cool down and think more rationally. Say, "I can see you are really upset. I am, too. I need to talk about this later. We can do it at three o'clock today or first thing tomorrow morning. Which do you prefer?"

Students still feel empowered because, once again, they have been asked to make a choice. However, once again, you are in charge as you delay the conversation. It's important to remember that students really need someone to be in charge. Yes, they want freedom, but they are happiest when it is within limits. This gives them the structure they so badly need. Too much freedom can result in chaos for them. It is like going to a department store that has a sale. You walk in and see tables all over saying, "50–80 percent off today." There are people pulling and poking all the products on the tables in their struggle to find bargains. It is chaos. Even as you reach in to look for your own bargain, you know that you would prefer to find the bargain another way—a way that had structure rather than chaos.

Changing the Frame

When students engage in a power struggle, they get stuck into continuing the struggle until they get what they want. Sometimes, by the time they get what they want, they do not really even care about what it was. Instead, it is about winning. Change this mental frame by distracting the student. Say something that is completely and totally different from what you both are talking about. For example, one day a youth was trying to get his teacher, Mrs. Carlton, in a power struggle. Mrs. Carlton suddenly turned to Brandon and said, "Oh my gosh! I think I left my garage door open this morning. I can't believe that it may be open. I wonder how I can get the garage door shut. My husband is at work, and I'm here. Oh my gosh!" Brandon stopped in his tracks and looked at Mrs. Carlton with a look that said, "Are you kidding?" She went on talking about her garage door, and Brandon walked away, forgetting all about the power struggle.

Mrs. Engle had her own way of handling power struggles. Mrs. Engle loved to sing. She would break out in a song in the middle of teaching. Her students loved her. She would make up words to songs to tie into teaching any concept. She did not plan the words ahead. She just got up there and taught and sang. She had complete command of the class's attention. They loved her. She was fun and entertaining as she taught. Raul was one of her students and was very strong willed. He got into trouble and had power struggles with all his other teachers, but he never got into trouble in Mrs. Engle's room. When asked about how she handled Raul, she said, "I sing." Whenever he begins to become argumentative, I either get the whole class singing a fun song, or I just look at him and start singing something. Mrs. Engle burst into song, "Not right now, Raul, not right now. Later, later, later. You can sing with me Raul, later, later, later." Raul always joined her in song, and they smiled and laughed, and the power struggle never happened. She had changed the frame with a song.

SKILL SEVEN: HOW TO HANDLE STUDENT CONFLICTS

Conflict in schools, as in life, is inevitable. Conflict occurs when two or more people have different views on a similar topic, and they not only disagree but try to convince the other person that their views are the correct ones. They confront each other often in unpleasant ways (Turnuklu, 2007). Instead, they need to learn to carefront. Carefrontation occurs when two or more people still disagree but discuss their disagreements in a caring way with each other.

Conflict occurs for varied reasons. Sometimes, it occurs because individuals lack social and communication interaction skills. One student may be struggling to say something, and it comes across to the other student as hostile or threatening. As soon as this occurs, the second student then retaliates by becoming hostile and even more threatening. Before you know it, a huge fight has sprouted from a really insignificant occurrence that became magnified.

Another reason that conflict may occur is when a student enters the classroom with displaced anger. Ethan was one of those students. He came into his fourth-grade classroom one day with a chip on his shoulder. What no one knew is that the night before his dad had left his mom. His mom had told Ethan that he was responsible. She said, "If only you had been better, he would not have left." Ethan felt like he was a bad person. He came to school the next day angry and hostile. When he and Gary were working together on a school project, Ethan became argumentative. Nothing Gary could do was right. Gary was a patient and quiet youth, but

Ethan kept picking on him. Gary got angrier and angrier, and, soon, he said some things back to Ethan—the conflict was on!

If Ethan had been able to come into school and talk about his feelings, this would all have been prevented. Instead, he came into school angry and hostile. His feelings escalated as the day went on, as he kept thinking about what had occurred the night before.

Strategies for Success for Student Conflicts

When people get angry, they confront each other and often say unpleasant things that they may later regret. They may become aggressive and even combative. Instead of confronting each other, it is better to "carefront" each other. In a "carefrontation," there is still a lack of agreement about a situation; however, the skills that are used to resolve the situation are caring skills.

Conflict resolution in general is not something that comes naturally. It is a skill that needs to be developed. Students need to learn this skill just like they learn their multiplication tables. Learning this skill may not help them get a better score on their state assessment, but it will help them get a better score in life and how they live it. It will also help make your classroom a better place, a safer place, a place in which students treat each other with respect. Take lots of time to teach this skill. Begin teaching it at the beginning of the school year and take time to periodically review it. There are many parts to teaching students conflict resolution through carefrontation.

I Statements—Four Parts

Typically when students are mad at each other, they make lots of "you statements." They say "You did ... and you did ..." "You statements" are accusatory and are almost guaranteed to get the other student upset and hostile. This promotes confrontation rather than carefrontation.

Teach students to use "I statements" (Heydenberk & Heydenberk, 2007). Instead of accusing one another of an inappropriate behavior, they say what they are feeling and ask for what they want. "I'm feeling upset. I want us to be friends. I need you to ... Is that OK with you?"

I statements during carefrontation have four parts:

1. Student's feeling: "I am feeling."
2. Goal statement: "I want us to be friends."
3. Statement of need: "I need you to ..."
4. Checking in: "Is that OK with you?"

1. Student's Feeling: "I am feeling."

   The first part, the student's feeling, is important for several reasons. First and foremost, it helps students acknowledge their own feelings. This is a major breakthrough for many students who have never learned to acknowledge their feelings. They go through life reacting to circumstances and shut down how they are feeling. The more they are in touch with their feelings, the more understanding of the feelings of others they can be. It is also important to acknowledge feelings because it lets others know what is happening inside the individual. There are times a student may be feeling hurt rather than really angry. Other students cannot read into the hearts and minds of their peers, but they can know what is occurring when they are told.

2. Goal Statement: "I want us to be friends."

   This second part is essential to carefrontation. It sets a mutual goal that both students can agree on. This paves the way to working through issues to get to the end goal. Most of the time, students will use the sample statement, "I want to be friends." This immediately adds warmth and caring to the issue and turns it into a carefrontation rather than a confrontation.

3. Statement of Need: "I need you to ..."

   This part does not talk about the incident that occurred. Actually, none of the parts of I statements address the incident. Instead, students ask for what they want and need. This is much more important than rehashing what already took place. That typically leads to more arguing and bickering. It becomes a confrontation rather than a carefrontation. This needs to be a brief and to-the-point statement. The words are always phrased in "I statements."

   - "I would appreciate if you would ..."
   - "I want you to ..."
   - "I need you to ..."

4. Checking In: "Is that OK with you?"

   When students check in to see if what they have said is OK with others, they are showing that they are respecting the rights of others. This is a key element in the process of carefrontation. The more others feel respect, the more they feel committed to the process of resolution.

It can happen that a student occasionally may say, "No, it is not OK with me." If this occurs, that student now uses the four parts to carefrontation, and the process begins again.

Rules for Carefrontation

This is an important process. In order to ensure success, there are rules all students must follow:

- They must always use the word "I" instead of the word "you."
- They have to stick to the issue and not bring up other issues.
- They cannot interrupt.
- They have to listen to the other person share.
- They always have to end with a handshake.

Book of Good Deeds

The opposite of conflict is community compassion. This is a tool that teaches students to be compassionate and caring. Every time students engage in acts of caring and compassion for others, write them in the book of good deeds. The book of good deeds is a class book that chronicles all of the good deeds that students do for each other. If you teach several classes, have a different one with a different cover for each class. Have the students elect an artist to design the cover. If students are older and capable of writing, have students take turns authoring the deeds. At the end of each class, students who have been helped by others tell the deed, and the author writes it down.

Peace Chain

Begin with a box of oval links cut from construction paper. Encourage your class to catch each other in acts of peace making. These include students choosing not to fight and students helping others who are upset to feel better. Each time an act of peace is reported, a link describing the act is added to a chain that starts at the ceiling. When the chain touches the floor, hold a celebration.

Role-Plays

Students need to be taught appropriate skills for communication. Do this through using role-playing activities. Use puppets to demonstrate social skills, including how to accept "no" for an answer. Have students get into dyads. One partner makes a request. The other partner responds, "No." The first student says, "OK," casually. Have them take turns practicing repeatedly making new requests, then hearing "no" and responding "OK."

Have them practice both giving and receiving compliments. There are students who never have said a nice word to another student. In fact they may not have ever said a nice word to another person at home either. Make sure they understand that it has to be sincere. If it is insincere, it feels worse than if nothing was said.

Teach them how to receive compliments. There are students who are more comfortable giving them than receiving them. These students may not feel worthy, or it may just be so foreign to them that they feel strange. Teach them to respond, "Thank you." Have them take turns giving and receiving compliments and responding, "Thank you."

Class Yellow Pages

This is a good way for students to link their common interests. Students complete a form about themselves. The form includes a list of their favorites. They list favorites like their favorite sports, favorite movie, favorite color, and favorite television program. Form dyads of students who share common interests. Do this on a weekly basis. The pairs work together on a project. The following week, pair other students together. Continue doing this until all students have worked together. This is an effective, fun way for students to get to know other students.

Figure 9.5 My Class Yellow Page

Name _____

Favorite movie _____

Favorite movie star _____

Favorite video game _____

Favorite television program _____

Favorite television star _____

Favorite food _____

Favorite color _____

Favorite hobby _____

Favorite sport _____

Favorite pet _____

Favorite vacation _____

Favorite weekend activity _____

Favorite game _____

Favorite book _____

Favorite day of year _____

Conclusion

I hope this book has made a difference in your life. More than that, I hope that it makes a difference in the lives of every student you teach. I want you to know how important you are. You truly are a difference maker. This poem is my concluding gift to you. It is called "You Believed in Me."

REMEMBER ME.

I am the one who caused you to have grey hairs.
I am the one who was your greatest challenge.
I am the one who was angry, defiant, difficult,
But even on my worst days,

YOU BELIEVED IN ME.

You knew that even though I was tough on the outside,
Inside, I needed you.

YOU BELIEVED IN ME.

I was ashamed because I couldn't control myself.
I was embarrassed because I knew I was different from everyone else.
I felt dumb, backwards, stupid, bad,
But on the outside—I sauntered, I talked back, I created disruptions.

But still, YOU BELIEVED IN ME.

And now, years later, I am taking this time
To tell you that because you saw through my behavior,
You did what changed my life forever:
You turned me from an angry, defiant child into who I am today.

YOU BELIEVED IN ME.

I graduated school instead of being a dropout.
I went on to achieve a wonderful career.
I am married and a parent.
I am a respected member of my community.
I try each day to give back what you gave me.

YOU BELIEVED IN ME and gave me hope.

THANK YOU.

And that is what you do for your students. You believe in them and give them hope.

Maryln Appelbaum

References

American Psychiatric Association. (2000). *Diagnostic and statistical manual of mental disorders* (4th ed.). Washington, DC: Author.

Anderson, C. A., & Bushman, B. J. (2001). Effects of violent video games on aggressive behavior, aggressive cognition, aggressive affect, physiological arousal, and prosocial behavior: A meta-analytic review of the scientific literature. *Psychological Science, 12,* 353–359.

Anderson, S. R., Campbell, S., & Cannon, B. O. (1994). The May Center for Early Childhood Education. In S. L. Harris & J. S. Handleman (Eds). *Preschool education programs for children with autism* (pp. 1536). Austin, TX: PROED

Azrin, N. H., Vinas, V., & Ehle, C. T. (2007). Physical activity as reinforcement for classroom calmness of ADHD children: A preliminary study. *Child & Family Behavior Therapy, 29*(2), 1–8.

Bagdi, A., & Pfister, I. K. (2006). Childhood Stressors and Coping Actions: A Comparison of Children and Parents' Perspectives. *Child and Youth Care Forum, 35*(1), 21–40.

Banks, R. (1997). Bullying in schools. Eric Digest. *Eric-RIEO, 19970401.*

Bausman, K., Bent, S., & Collister, J. (1999). Improving social skills at the elementary and secondary level. *Eric,* 62 pp. (ED433099)

Beane, A. (1999). Fostering a bully-free classroom. *Curriculum Review, 39,* 4.

Bettman, J. (2000). Nurturing the respectful community through practical life. *NAMTA Journal, 25*(1), 101–116.

Biederman, J., Mick, E., Faraone, S. V., Spencer, T., Wilens, T. E., & Wozniak, J. (2000). Pediatric mania: A developmental subtype of bipolar disorder? *Biological Psychiatry, 48,* 458–466.

Bowman, R., Carr, T., Cooper, K., Miles, R., & Toner, T. (1998). *Innovative Strategies for Unlocking Difficult Children.* Chapin, SC: YouthLight, Inc.

Brown, M. S., Ilderton, P., Taylor, A., & Lock, R. H. (2001). Include a student with an attention problem in the General Education Classroom. *Intervention in School & Clinic, 34*(1), 50–53.

Bullies and their victims. (2001). *Harvard Mental Health Letter, 18,* 4–7.

Carney, A. G., & Merrell, K. W. (2001). *School Psychology International, 22,* 364–382.

Carroll, A., Houghton, S., Taylor, M., Hemingway, F., List-Kerz, M., Cordin, R., & Douglas, G. (2006). Responding to interpersonal and physically provoking situations in classrooms: Emotional intensity in children with attention deficit hyperactivity disorder. *International Journal of Disability, Development & Education, 53*(2), 209–227.

Carter, A. S., & O'Donnell, D. A. (2000). Social and emotional adjustment in children affected with Gilles de la Tourette's syndrome: Associations with ADHD and family functioning. *Journal of Child Psychology & Psychiatry & Allied Disciplines, 41*(2), 215–223.

Charney, R. S. (1998). Got the "kids who blurt out" blues? *Instructor-Intermediate, 107*(6), 90–93.

Cumine, V., Dunlop, J., & Stevenson, G. (2005). *Asperger syndrome, a practical guide for teachers.* London: David Fulton Publishers.

Denson, T. F., Pedersen, W. C., & Miller, N. (2006). The displaced aggression questionnaire. *Journal of Personality & Social Psychology, 90*(6), 1032–1051.

Dess, N. K. (2001). Saved by the bell? Serious science brings hope to victims and bullies. *Psychology Today, 34*, 47.

Dettmer, S., Simpson, I., Myles, B. S., & Ganz, J. B. (2000). The use of visual supports to facilitate transitions of students with autism. *Focus on Autism and Other Developmental Disabilities, 15*, 163–169.

Duffy, A. (2007). Does bipolar disorder exist in children: A selected review. *Canadian Journal of Psychiatry, 52*(7), 409–417.

Egel, A. (1981). Reinforcer variation: Implications for motivating developmentally disabled children. *Journal of Applied Behavior Analysis, 14*, 345–350.

Fine, L. (2002). Study: Minimum ADHD incidence is 7.5 percent. *Education Week, 21*(28), 10.

Ferko, D. K. (2005). Proactively address challenging behaviors. *Intervention in School & Clinic, 41*(1), 30–31.

Frank, K. (2001). *ADHD: 102 practical strategies for "reducing the deficit."* Chapin, SC: YouthLight, Inc.

Garrity, C., & Jens, K. (1997). Bully proofing your school: Creating a positive climate. *Intervention in School & Clinic, 32*, 235–244.

Gartrell, D. (2007). Tattling: It drives teachers bonkers. *Young Children, 62*(1), 46–48.

Gillberg, C. (2003). ADHD and DAMP: A general health perspective. *Child & Adolescent Mental Health, 8*(3), 106–113.

Gunter, P. L., & Shores, R. E. (1995). On the move: Using teacher/student proximity to improve students' behavior. *Teaching Exceptional Children, 28*(1), 12–15.

Hallam, S., Price, J., & Katsarou, G. (2002). The effects of background music on primary school pupils' task performance. *Educational Studies, 28*(2), 111–122.

Harris, K. R., Friedlander, B. D., Saddler, B., Frizzelle, R., & Graham, S. (2005). Self-monitoring of attention versus self-monitoring of academic performance: Effects among students with ADHD in the General Education classroom. *Journal of Special Education, 39*(3), 145–156.

Heflin, L. J, & Alberto, P. A. (2001). Establishing a behavioral context for learning for students with autism. *Focus on Autism & Other Developmental Disabilities, 16*, 93–102.

Heydenberk, W., & Heydenberk, R. (2007). More than manners: Conflict resolution in primary level classrooms. *Early Childhood Education Journal, 35*(2), 119–126.

Hipsky, S. (2007). Differentiated instruction: Flexibility without breaking. *Essays in Education, 19,* 96–99.

Jenson, E. (2000). *Brain-based learning.* San Diego, CA: Brain Store, Inc.

Jepson, B. (2007). *Changing the course of autism: A scientific approach for parents and physicians.* Boulder, CO: Sentient Publications.

Jimenez, K. (2000). Is your child more than a handful? *Pediatrics for Parents, 18,* 3–4.

Kendall, P. C., & Treadwell, K. R. H. (2007). The role of self-statements as a mediator in treatment for youth with anxiety disorders. *Journal of Consulting & Clinical Psychology, 75*(3), 380–389.

Leslie, L. K., Weckerly, J., Plemmons, D., Landsyerk, J., & Eastman, S. (2004). Implementing the American Academy of Pediatrics Attention-Deficit Hyperactivity Disorder diagnostic guidelines in primary care settings. *Pediatrics, 114*(1), 129–140.

Lincoln, A. J., Courchesne, E., Harms, L., & Allen, M. (1995). Sensory modulation of auditory stimuli in children with autism and receptive developmental language disorder: Event-related brain potential evidence. *Journal of Autism and Developmental Disorders, 25,* 521–539.

Munk, D. D., & Repp, A. C. (1994). The relationship between instructional variables and problem behavior: A review. *Exceptional Children, 60,* 390–401.

Overstreet, S. (2000). Exposure to community violence: Defining the problem and understanding the consequences. *Journal of Child & Family Studies, 9*(1), 7–25.

Parish, T., & Mahoney, S. (2006). Classrooms: How to turn them from battlegrounds to connecting places. *Education, 126*(3), 437–440.

Parker, H. C. (2005). *The ADHD handbook for schools: Effective strategies for identifying and teaching students with attention-deficit/hyperactivity disorder.* Plantation, FL: Specialty Press, Inc.

Prizant, B. M., & Rubin, E. (1999). Contemporary issues in interventions for autism spectrum disorders: A commentary. *JASH, 24,* 199–208.

Purcell, J. (1999). Children, adolescents, and obsessive compulsive disorder in the classroom. *Eric,* 22 pp. (ED445439)

Reiter, J. (2004). Recognizing and treating adults with attention deficit hyperactivity disorder. *Psychiatric Times, 21 (Supplement),* 1–4.

Rowe, C. (2003). Albert Einstein, Andy Kaufman, and Andy Warhol: The controversial disorder they may have shared. *Biography, 7*(12), 86–114.

Skinner, C. H., Cashwell, T. H., & Skinner, A. L. (2000). Increased tootling: The effects of a peer-monitored group contingency program on students' reports of peers' prosocial behaviors. *Psychology in the Schools, 37*(3), 263–271.

Smith, S. (2001). Stephen W. Smith: Strategies for building a positive classroom environment by preventing behavior problems. *Intervention in School & Clinic, 37,* 31–36.

Stearns, C., Dunham, M., McIntosh, D., & Dean, R. S. (2004). Attention deficit hyperactivity disorder and working memory in clinically referred adults. *International Journal of Neuroscience, 114*(2), 273–287.

Stolzer, J. M. (2007). The ADHD epidemic in America. *Ethical Human Psychology & Psychiatry, 9*(2), 109–116.

Stuart, S. K., Flis, L. D., & Rinaldi, C. (2006). Connecting with families: Parents speak up about preschool services for their children with autism spectrum disorders. *Teaching Exceptional Children, 39*(1), 46–51.

Turnuklu, A. (2007). Students' conflicts: Causes, resolution strategies, and tactics in high schools. *Educational Administration: Theory & Practice, 49,* 159–166.

Valas, H. (2001). Learned helplessness and psychological adjustment II: Effects of learning disabilities and low achievement. *Scandinavian Journal of Educational Research, 45*(2), 101–114.

Wagner, C. (1985). *Color power.* Chicago: Wagner Institute for Color Research.

Walker, M. (1991). *The power of color,* New York: Avery Publishing Group.

Winebrenner, S. (2006). *Teaching kids with learning difficulties in the regular classroom: Ways to challenge and motivate struggling students to achieve proficiency with required standards.* Minneapolis, MN: Spirit Press.

Index

CORWIN PRESS

The Corwin Press logo—a raven striding across an open book—represents the union of courage and learning. Corwin Press is committed to improving education for all learners by publishing books and other professional development resources for those serving the field of PreK–12 education. By providing practical, hands-on materials, Corwin Press continues to carry out the promise of its motto: **"Helping Educators Do Their Work Better."**

Appelbaum
Training Institute

Appelbaum Training Institute (ATI) provides the latest, the best, and the most research-based information on the most current subjects in a fun and enjoyable manner through professional development, training, and resources to educators and parents of children of all ages and diverse backgrounds. The ATI motto is **"Building Bridges to the Future,"** and that is exactly what the Appelbaum Training Institute does every day in every way for educators across the world.